ac.   **Thermoplastic rooflights:** limitations on the use of thermoplastics rooflights take account of the new classification system for thermoplastics.

B5

ad.   **Fire services:** there is a new requirement for access and facilities, supported by guidance on the provision of vehicle and personnel access, water mains and basement venting.

The amendments issued in the Amendments 1992 document have been incorporated in this reprinting, of the 1992 edition of the Approved Document.

B

Contents

B

DIAGRAMS

Use of Guidance

THE APPROVED DOCUMENTS

The Building Regulations 1991, which come into operation on 1 June 1992, replace the Building Regulations 1985 (SI 1985 No. 1065) and consolidate all subsequent revisions to those regulations. This document is one of a series that has been approved by the Secretary of State as practical guidance on meeting the requirements of Schedule 1 and regulation 7 of the Building Regulations.

At the back of this document is a list of those documents currently published by the Department of the Environment and the Welsh Office which have been approved for the purpose of the Building Regulations 1991.

The detailed provisions contained in the Approved Documents are intended to provide guidance for some of the more common building situations. In other circumstances, alternative ways of demonstrating compliance with the requirements may be appropriate.

Evidence supporting compliance

There is no obligation to adopt any particular solution contained in an Approved Document if you prefer to meet the relevant requirement in some other way. However, should a contravention of a requirement be alleged then, if you have followed the guidance in the relevant Approved Documents, that will be evidence tending to show that you have complied with the regulations. If you have not followed the guidance then that will be evidence tending to show that you have not complied. It will then be for you to demonstrate by other means that you have satisfied the requirement.

Other requirements

The guidance contained in an Approved Document relates only to the particular requirements of the Regulations which that document addresses. The building work will also have to comply with the Requirements of any other relevant paragraphs in Schedule 1 to the Regulations. There are Approved Documents which give guidance on each of the other requirements in Schedule 1 and on regulation 7.

LIMITATION ON REQUIREMENTS

In accordance with regulation 8, the requirements in Parts A to K and N of Schedule 1 to the Building Regulations do not require anything to be done except for the purpose of securing reasonable standards of health and safety for persons in or about the building.

MATERIALS AND WORKMANSHIP

Any building work which is subject to requirements imposed by Schedule 1 of the Building Regulations should, in accordance with regulation 7, be carried out with proper materials and in a workmanlike manner.

You may show that you have complied with regulation 7 in a number of ways, for example, by the appropriate use of a product bearing an EC mark in accordance with the Construction Products Directive (89/106/EEC), or by following an appropriate technical specification (as defined in that Directive), a British Standard, a British Board of Agrément Certificate, or an alternative national technical specification of any member state of the European Community which, in use, is equivalent. You will find further guidance in the Approved Document supporting regulation 7 on materials and workmanship.

Technical specifications

Building Regulations are made for specific purposes; health and safety, energy conservation and the welfare and convenience of disabled people. Standards and technical approvals are relevant guidance to the extent that they relate to these considerations. However, they may also address other aspects of performance such as serviceability or aspects which although they relate to health and safety are not covered by the Regulations.

When an approved document makes reference to a named standard, the relevant version of the standard is the one listed at the end of the publication. However, if this version of the standard has been revised or updated by the issuing standards body, the new version may be used as a source of guidance provided it continues to address the relevant requirements of the Regulations.

The Secretary of State has agreed with the British Board of Agrément on the aspects of performance which it needs to assess in preparing its Certificates in order that the Board may demonstrate the compliance of a product or system which has an Agrément Certificate with the requirements of the Regulations. An Agrément Certificate issued by the Board under these arrangements will give assurance that the product or system to which the Certificate relates, if properly used in accordance with the terms of the Certificate, will meet the relevant requirements.

Similarly, the appropriate use of a product which complies with a European Technical Approval as defined in the Construction Products Directive will also meet the relevant requirements.

General Introduction

FIRE SAFETY

Arrangement of Sections

0.1 The provisions set out in this document, under B1 to B5, deal with different aspects of fire safety, with the following aims:

B1: that there is a satisfactory standard of means of escape for persons in the event of fire in a building.

B2: that fire spread over the internal linings of buildings is inhibited.

B3: to ensure the stability of buildings in the event of fire: to ensure that there is a sufficient degree of fire separation within buildings and between adjoining buildings; and to inhibit the unseen spread of fire and smoke in concealed spaces in buildings.

B4: that external walls and roofs have adequate resistance to the spread of fire in the external envelope, and that spread of fire from one building to another is restricted.

B5: to ensure satisfactory access for fire appliances to buildings and the provision of facilities in buildings to assist fire fighters in the saving of life of people in and around buildings.

0.2 Whilst guidance appropriate to each of these aspects is set out separately in this document, many of the provisions are closely interlinked. For example, there is a close link between the provisions for means of escape (B1) and those for the control of fire growth (B2), fire containment (B3), and facilities for the fire service (B5). Similarly there are links between B3 and the provisions for controlling external fire spread (B4), and between B3 and B5. Interaction between these different requirements should be recognised where variations in the standard of provision are being considered. A higher standard under one of the requirements may be of benefit in respect of one or more of the other requirements. The guidance in the document as a whole should be considered as a package aimed at achieving an acceptable standard of fire safety.

0.3 In the guidance on B1 the provisions for dwellings are separated from those for all other types of building, because there are important differences in the approach that has been adopted. Dwellinghouses (Section 1) pose different problems from flats and maisonettes, which are therefore treated separately in Section 2.

Provisions common to more than one of Part B's requirements

0.4 Under the guidance on each requirement in this publication there are a number of items that are common to one or more of the requirements. These include:

A. fire performance of materials and structures;

B. provisions regarding fire doors;

C. methods of measurement;

D. a classification of purpose groups;

E. definitions.

For convenience these items have been drawn together for common reference in appendices at the end.

Purpose groups

0.5 Much of the guidance in this document is related to the use of the building. The use classifications are termed purpose groups, and they are described in Appendix D.

Fire performance of protection systems, materials and structures.

0.6 Much of the guidance throughout this publication is given in terms of performance in relation to standard fire test methods. Details are drawn together in Appendix A to which reference is made where appropriate. In the case of fire protection systems reference is made to standards for systems design and installation.

Fire doors

0.7 Guidance in respect of fire doors is set out in Appendix B.

Methods of measurement

0.8 Some form of measurement is an integral part of much of the guidance in this publication, and methods are set out in Appendix C. Aspects of measurement specific to means of escape are covered in the introduction to B1 (paragraphs 0.37 et seq).

Definitions

0.9 The definitions are given in Appendix E.

Fire safety engineering

0.10 A fire safety engineering approach that takes into account the total fire safety package can provide an alternative approach to fire safety. It may be the only viable way to achieve a satisfactory standard of fire safety in some large and complex buildings.

0.11 Some variation of the provisions set out in this document may also be appropriate where Part B applies to existing buildings, and particularly in buildings of special architectural or historic interest, where rigid compliance with the guidance in this document might prove unduly restrictive. In such cases it would be appropriate to take into account a range of fire safety features, some of which are dealt with in this document, and some of which are not addressed in any detail, and to set these against an assessment of the hazard and risk peculiar to the particular case.

0.12 Factors that should be taken into account include:

a. the anticipated risk of a fire occurring

b. the anticipated fire severity

c. the ability of a structure to resist the spread of fire and smoke

d. the consequential danger to people in and around the building

0.13 A wide variety of measures could be considered and incorporated to a greater or lesser extent, as appropriate in the circumstances. These include:

a. the adequacy of means to prevent fire

b. early fire warning by an automatic detection and warning system

c. the standard of means of escape

d. provision of smoke control

e. control of the rate of growth of a fire

f. the adequacy of the structure to resist the effects of a fire

g. the degree of fire containment

h. fire separation between buildings or parts of buildings

j. the standard of active measures for fire extinguishment or control

k. facilities to assist the fire service

l. availability of powers to require staff training in fire safety and fire routines, e.g. under the Fire Precautions Act 1971 Chapter 40 or registration or licensing procedures

m. consideration of the availability of any continuing control under other legislation that could ensure continued maintenance of such systems

0.14 It is possible to use quantitative techniques to evaluate risk and hazard. Some factors in the measures listed above can be given numerical values in some circumstances. The assumptions made when quantitative methods are used need careful assessment.

0.15 An example of an overall approach to fire safety can be found in BS 5588: *Fire precautions in the design, construction and use of buildings Part 10: Code of practice for shopping complexes*, which is referred to in Section 11. Similarly a building containing an atrium penetrating compartment floors may need special fire safety measures.

Property protection
0.16 Building Regulations are intended to ensure that a reasonable standard of safety is provided, in case of fire. The protection of property, including the building itself, may require additional measures, and insurers will in general seek their own higher standards, before accepting the insurance risk.

Material alteration
0.17 There are no powers under Building Regulations for standards set by the Regulations to be maintained over the life of the building. However an alteration which results in a building being less satisfactory in relation to compliance with the requirements of Parts B1, B3, B4 or B5, than it was before, is controllable under Regulations 3 (meaning of building work) and 4 (requirements relating to building work) of The Building Regulations 1991, as a material alteration.

The Requirement

This Approved Document, which takes effect on 1 June 1992, deals with the following requirement from Part B of Schedule 1 to the Building Regulations 1991:

Requirement	Limits on application
Means of escape **B1**. The building shall be designed and constructed so that there are means of escape in case of fire from the building to a place of safety outside the building capable of being safely and effectively used at all material times.	Requirement B1 does not apply to any prison provided under section 33 of The Prisons Act 1952 (power to provide prisons etc.).

Guidance

Performance

In the Secretary of State's view the requirement of B1 will be met if:

a. there are routes of sufficient number and capacity, which are suitably located to enable persons to escape to a place of safety in the event of fire;

b. the routes are sufficiently protected from the effects of fire by enclosure where necessary;

c. the routes are adequately lit;

d. the exits are suitably signed; and if

e. there are appropriate facilities to either limit the ingress of smoke to the escape route(s) or suitable measures are taken to restrict the fire and remove smoke; all to an extent necessary depending on the use of the building, its size and height.

Introduction

0.18* These provisions relate to building work and material changes of use which are subject to the functional requirement B1, and they may therefore affect new or existing buildings. They are concerned with the measures necessary to ensure reasonable facilities for means of escape in case of fire. They are only concerned with structural fire precautions where these are necessary to safeguard escape routes.

They assume that in the design of the building, reliance should not be placed on external rescue by the fire service. The document has been prepared on the basis that, in an emergency, the occupants of any part of a building should be able to escape safely without any external assistance.

Special considerations, however, apply to some institutional buildings in which the principle of evacuation without assistance is not practical.

It should also be noted that the guidance for 1 and 2 storey dwellings is limited to the provision of openable windows for emergency egress in certain situations, and to the provision of smoke alarms.

0.19 Attention is drawn to the fact that there may be other legislation imposing requirements for means of escape in case of fire with which the building must comply, and which operates when the building is brought into use. The main legislation in this area is the Fire Precautions Act 1971, generally enforced by the fire authority, which provides for the designation of certain uses of premises for which a fire

* Introductory paragraphs 0.1 - 0.17 are on pages 7 and 8

certificate is required and, in the case of certain smaller premises, imposes a statutory duty on the occupiers to provide reasonable means of escape in case of fire.

Although there is no requirement under the building regulations to provide a means of giving warning in case of fire, the provision of an appropriate warning system is an essential element in the overall strategy for fire safety in an occupied building. Most places of work, many public assembly buildings and institutional and residential care buildings, will be subject to a requirement under other legislation, to provide appropriate means of giving warning in case of fire. British Standard 5839: Part 1 gives guidance on suitable fire warning for various uses of premises.

Interaction with other legislation

0.20 Under the Fire Precautions Act, unless there are regulations made under Section 12 of that Act (and it is necessary to make requirements to satisfy those regulations), fire authorities cannot as a condition for issuing a fire certificate, make requirements for structural or other alterations relating to escape, if the plans of the building comply with building regulations. However if the fire authority is satisfied that the means of escape in case of fire are inadequate by reason of matters concerning particulars which were not required to be supplied to the local authority, in connection with the deposit of plans for building regulation purposes, then the fire authority is not barred from making requirements.

In addition it should be noted that there are some things that may be required under the Fire Precautions Act that are outside the scope of the building regulations. One example is the provision of first aid fire fighting equipment, for use by the occupants.

0.21 Under the Health and Safety at Work etc Act 1974 the Health and Safety Executive may have similar responsibilities for certification in the case of highly specialised industrial and storage premises.

0.22 Under the Housing Act 1985 the local authority is obliged to require means of escape in case of fire in certain types of houses which are occupied by persons not forming a single household (Houses in Multiple Occupation).

However, compliance with the guidance in this document will enable a newly constructed or converted House in Multiple Occupation to achieve an acceptable standard of fire safety.

0.23 There are a number of other Statutes enforced by the local authority or the fire authority that may be applied to premises of specific uses once they are occupied.

Management of premises
0.24 This document has been written on the assumption that the building concerned will be properly managed. Failure to take proper management responsibility may result in the prosecution of a building owner or occupier under legislation such as the Fire Precautions Act or the Health and Safety at Work etc Act, and/or prohibition of the use of the premises.

Analysis of the problem

0.25 The design of means of escape should take into account the form of the building and activities of the occupants, the likelihood of fire, potential sources of fire and the potential for fire spread through the building.

0.26 Fires do not normally start in two different places in a building at the same time. Initially a fire will create a hazard only in the part in which it starts and it is unlikely, at this stage, to involve a large area. The fire may subsequently spread to other parts of the building, usually along the circulation routes. The items that are the first to be ignited are often furnishings and other items not controlled by the regulations. It is less likely that the fire will originate in the structure of the building itself and the risk of it originating accidentally in circulation areas, such as corridors, lobbies or stairways, is limited, provided that the combustible content of such areas is restricted.

0.27 The primary danger associated with fire in its early stages is not flame but the smoke and noxious gases produced by the fire. They cause most of the casualties and may also obscure the way to escape routes and exits. Measures designed to provide safe means of escape must therefore limit the rapid spread of smoke and fumes.

Criteria for means of escape
0.28 The basic principles for the design of means of escape are:

a.   that there should be alternative means of escape from most situations;

b.   where direct escape to a place of safety is not possible, it should be possible to reach a place of relative safety, such as a protected stairway, which is on a route to an exit, within a reasonable travel distance. In such cases the means of escape will consist of two parts, the first being unprotected in accommodation and circulation areas, and the second in protected stairways (and in some circumstances protected corridors).

The ultimate place of safety is the open air clear of the effects of the fire. However, in modern buildings which are large and complex, reasonable safety may be reached within the building, provided suitable planning and protection measures are incorporated.

0.29 The following are not acceptable as means of escape:

a.   lifts (except for a suitably designed and installed evacuation lift that may be used for the evacuation of disabled people, in a fire);

b.   portable ladders and throw-out ladders; and

c.   manipulative apparatus and appliances: eg fold down ladders.

Escalators should not be counted as providing protected stair capacity, although it is recognised that they are likely to be used by people who are escaping. Mechanised walkways could be accepted, and their capacity assessed on the basis of their use as a walking route, while in the static mode .

Alternative means of escape
0.30 There is always the possibility of the path of a single escape route being rendered impassable by fire, smoke or fumes and, ideally, people should be able to turn their backs on a fire wherever it occurs and travel away from it to a final exit or protected escape route leading to a place of safety. However in certain conditions a single direction of escape (a dead end) can be accepted as providing reasonable safety. These conditions depend on the use of the building and its associated fire risk, the size and height of the building, the extent of the dead end, and the numbers of persons accommodated within the dead end.

Unprotected and protected escape routes
0.31 The unprotected part of an escape route is that part which a person has to traverse before reaching either the safety of a final exit or the comparative safety of a protected escape route.

Unprotected escape routes should be limited in extent so that people do not have to travel excessive distances while exposed to the immediate danger of fire and smoke.

Even with protected horizontal escape routes the distance to a final exit or protected stairway needs to be limited because the structure does not give protection indefinitely.

0.32 Protected stairways are designed to provide virtually 'fire sterile' areas which lead to places of safety outside the building. Once inside a protected stairway, a person can be considered to be safe from immediate danger from flame and smoke. They can then proceed to a place of safety at their own pace. To enable this to be done, flames, smoke and gases must be excluded from these escape routes, as far as is reasonably possible, by fire resisting structures or by an appropriate smoke control system, or by a combination of both these methods. This does not preclude the use of unprotected stairs for day-to-day circulation, but these "accommodation" stairs can only play a very limited role in terms of means of escape.

Means of escape for disabled people

0.33 Part M of the Regulations, Access and facilities for disabled people, requires reasonable provision for access by disabled people to certain buildings, or parts of buildings. However it may not be necessary to incorporate special structural measures to aid means of escape for the disabled. Management arrangements to provide assisted escape may be all that is necessary. BS 5588 *Fire precautions in the design and construction of buildings: Part 8:1988 Code of practice for means of escape for disabled people,* gives guidance on means of escape for disabled people. It introduces the concept of refuges and the use of an evacuation lift, and stresses the need for effective management of the evacuation.

Health care premises

0.34 In parts of hospitals designed to be used by patients, and in similar accommodation such as nursing homes and homes for the elderly, where there are people who are bed-ridden or who have very restricted mobility, the principle of total evacuation of a building in the event of fire may be inappropriate. It is also unrealistic to suppose that all patients will leave without assistance.

In this and other ways the specialised nature of some health care premises demands a different approach to the provision of means of escape, from much of that embodied by the guidance in this Approved Document.

The Department of Health has prepared a set of guidance documents on fire precautions in Health Care buildings, under the general title of *"Firecode"*, taking into account the particular characteristics of these buildings. The provision of means of escape in new hospitals should therefore follow the guidance in the appropriate section of Firecode (either *'Nucleus Fire Precautions Recommendations'* or Health Technical Memorandum 81). Where work to existing hospitals including NHS hospitals and NHS Trust hospitals is concerned with means of escape, the guidance in the Home Office *Draft Guide to Fire Precautions in Hospitals* should be followed. Attention is also drawn to the *Draft guide to fire precautions in existing residential care premises.*

Where an existing house of one or two storeys is converted for use as an unsupervised Group Home for not more than 7 mentally handicapped or mentally ill people, it should be regarded as a purpose group 1(c) building if the means of escape are provided in accordance with Health Technical Memorandum 88.

It should be noted that Firecode contains managerial and other fire safety provisions which are outside the scope of building regulations.

Security

0.35 The need for easy and rapid evacuation of a building in case of fire may conflict with the control of entry and exit in the interest of security. Measures intended to prevent unauthorised access can also hinder entry of the fire service to rescue people trapped by fire.

Potential conflicts should be identified and resolved at the design stage and not left to ad hoc expedients after completion. The architectural liaison officers attached to most police forces are a valuable source of advice.

Use of the document

0.36 Sections 1 & 2 deal with dwellings and Sections 3 & 4 with buildings other than dwellings. Section 1 is about dwellinghouses and Section 2 is on flats and maisonettes. Section 3 concerns the design of means of escape on one level (the horizontal phase in multi-storey buildings). Section 4 deals with stairways and the vertical phase of the escape route. Section 5 gives guidance on matters common to all parts of the means of escape, other than in houses.

Methods of measurement

0.37 The following methods of measurement apply specifically to B1. Other aspects of measurement applicable to Part B in general are given in Appendix C.

Occupant capacity

0.38 the occupant capacity is defined as follows:

i. **occupant capacity of a room or storey** is the maximum number of persons it is designed to hold (where this is known) or: the number calculated (using the floor space factors given in Table 1) by dividing the area of room or storey (m²) by the floor space per person (m²).

Note: 'area' excludes stair enclosures, lifts and sanitary accommodation.

ii. **occupant capacity of a building or part of a building** is the sum of the number of occupants of the storeys in the building or part.

Travel distance

0.39 Travel distance is measured by way of the shortest route, which if:

i. there is fixed seating or other fixed obstructions, is along the centre line of the seatways and gangways;

ii. it includes a stair, is along the pitch line on the centre line of travel.

Width

0.40 The width of:

i. **a door (or doorway)** is the width of the opening door leaf (or the sum of the widths of both opening door leaves in the case of double doors). Note: It is not the clear width between door stops.

ii. **an escape route** is the width at 1.5m above floor or stair pitch line when defined by walls (handrails fixed to walls may be ignored) or, elsewhere, the minimum width of passage available between any fixed obstructions;

iii. **a stair** is the clear width between the walls or balustrades but stringers and handrails intruding not more than 30 mm and 100mm respectively may be ignored.

Table 1 Floor space factors

	Type of accommodation (1)(6)	Floor space factor m²/person
1.	Standing spectator areas	0.3
2.	Amusement arcade, Assembly hall (including a general purpose place of assembly) Bar (including a lounge bar), Bingo hall, Dance floor or hall, Club, Crush hall, Venue for pop concert and similar events, Queuing area	0.5
3.	Concourse or shopping mall (2)	0.75
4.	Committee room, Common room, Conference room, Dining room, Licensed betting office (public area), Lounge (other than a lounge bar), Meeting room, Reading room, Restaurant, Staff room, Waiting room (3)	1.0
5.	Exhibition hall	1.5
6.	Shop sales area (4), Skating rink	2.0
7.	Art gallery, Dormitory, Factory production area, Office (open-plan exceeding 60m²) Workshop	5.0
8.	Kitchen, Library, Office (other than in 7 above), Shop sales area (5)	7.0
9.	Bedroom or Study-bedroom	8.0
10.	Bed-sitting room, Billiards room	10.0
11.	Storage and warehousing	30.0
12.	Car park	two persons per parking space

Notes:

1. Where accommodation is not directly covered by the descriptions given, a reasonable value based on a similar use may be selected.

2. Refer to section 4 of BS 5588: Part 10 for detailed guidance on the calculation of occupancy in common public areas in shopping complexes.

3. Alternatively the occupant capacity may be taken as the number of fixed seats provided, if the occupants will normally be seated.

4. Shops excluding those under item 8, but including - supermarkets and department stores (all sales areas), shops for personal services such as hairdressing and shops for the delivery or collection of goods for cleaning, repair or other treatment or for members of the public themselves carrying out such cleaning, repair or other treatment.

5. Shops (excluding those in covered shopping complexes, and excluding department stores) trading predominantly in furniture, floor coverings, cycles, prams, large domestic appliances or other bulky goods, or trading on a wholesale self-selection basis (cash and carry).

6. If there is to be mixed use, the most onerous factor(s) should be applied.

Section 1

DWELLINGHOUSES

1.1 The means of escape from a one or two storey house are simple, and few provisions are specified in this section beyond ensuring that each habitable room either opens directly onto a hallway or stair leading to the entrance, or that it has a window or door through which escape could be made, and that means are provided for giving early warning in the event of fire. With increasing height more complex provisions are needed because escape through upper windows becomes increasingly hazardous. It is then necessary to protect the internal stairway. If there are floors more than 7.5 m above ground level, the risk that the stairway will become impassable before occupants of the upper parts of the house have escaped is appreciable, and an alternative route from those parts is called for.

1.2 In providing fire protection of any kind in houses it should be recognised that measures which significantly interfere with the day-to-day convenience of the occupants may be less reliable in the long term.

1.3 This guidance is also applicable to houses, which are considered to be "houses in multiple occupation". A house in multiple occupation is defined in section 345 of the Housing Act 1985 as "a house which is occupied by persons who do not form a single household". Guidance on the interpretation of this wide-ranging definition is given in the joint Department of the Environment/Home Office/Welsh Office Circular (DoE 12/86; HO 39/86; WO 23/86) "Memorandum on overcrowding and houses in multiple occupation".

General provisions

Automatic smoke detection and alarms

1.4 In most dwelling houses the installation of self-contained smoke alarms or automatic fire detection and alarm systems, can significantly increase the level of safety by automatically giving an early warning of fire.

1.5 If dwellings are not protected by an automatic fire detection and alarm system in accordance with the relevant recommendations of BS 5839: Part 1 to at least an L3 standard, they should be provided with a suitable number of mains operated self-contained smoke alarms which conform to BS 5446: Part 1, installed in accordance with the following guidance in paragraph 1.8 et seq. The smoke alarms may be wholly mains operated or mains operated with a secondary power supply such as batteries. Smoke alarms operated by primary batteries are not acceptable (see note to clause 23, BS 5446: Part 1: 1990).

Large dwellinghouses

1.6 Self-contained smoke alarms are not considered suitable for very large dwellings. If the circulation route from one room to another at any one level is more than 30m long (ie. the distance from any part of one room to the most distant part of any other room on that floor), a system of discrete detectors and alarms connected to a control and indicating unit, all conforming to at least the L3 standard of BS 5839: Part 1 should be installed.

Sheltered housing

1.7 The detection equipment in dwellinghouses which are part of a sheltered housing scheme with a warden or supervisor, should have a connection to a central monitoring point so that the person in charge (or central alarm relay station) is aware that a fire has been detected in one of the dwellings, and can identify the dwelling concerned. These provisions are not intended to be applied to the common parts of a sheltered housing development, such as communal lounges, or to sheltered accommodation in the Institutional or Other residential purpose groups.

Installations based on self-contained smoke alarms

1.8 Self-contained smoke alarms should be positioned in the circulation areas. They should be near enough to places where fires are most likely to start (eg kitchen or living room) to pick up smoke in the early stages, while also being close enough to bedroom doors for the alarm to be effective when occupants are asleep.

1.9 There should be a self-contained smoke alarm within 7m of the doors to rooms where a fire is likely to start (the kitchen or living room), and within 3m of bedroom doors. These distances are measured horizontally. A corridor which is over 15m long should have more than one self-contained smoke alarm.

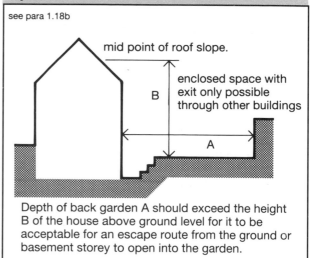

Diagram 1 **Conditions for it to be acceptable for a ground or basement storey exit to lead into an enclosed space**

see para 1.18b

mid point of roof slope.

enclosed space with exit only possible through other buildings

B

A

Depth of back garden A should exceed the height B of the house above ground level for it to be acceptable for an escape route from the ground or basement storey to open into the garden.

1.10 Where more than one self-contained smoke alarm is installed they should be interconnected so that detection of smoke by any one unit operates the alarm signal in all of them. The manufacturers' instructions about the maximum number of alarms that can be interconnected should be followed

1.11 In a dwellinghouse which has accommodation on more than one storey there should be at least one self-contained smoke alarm on each of these storeys, and they should all be interconnected.

1.12 Self-contained smoke alarms should be permanently wired to a separately fused circuit at the distribution board. They may operate at a low voltage via a mains transformer. Cable for the power supply to, and interconnection of, self-contained smoke alarms need have no special fire-survival properties. The wiring installation should conform to the IEE Wiring Regulations.

1.13 Each self contained smoke alarm should be fixed to the ceiling at least 300mm from any wall or light fitting. A central position is preferable. Units designed for wall mounting should be fixed between 150 and 300mm below the ceiling. The method of fixing should be in accordance with the manufacturer's instructions.

1.14 It should be possible to reach the self-contained smoke alarms to carry out routine maintenance, such as testing and cleaning, easily and safely. For this reason self-contained smoke alarms should not be fixed over a stair shaft or any other opening between floors.

1.15 Self-contained smoke alarms should not be fixed next to or directly above heaters or air conditioning outlets. They should not be fixed in bathrooms, showers, cooking areas or garages, or any other place where steam, condensation or fumes could give false alarms.

Self-contained smoke alarms should not be fitted in places that get very hot (such as a boiler room), or very cold (such as an unheated porch). They should not be fixed to surfaces which are normally much warmer or colder than the rest of the space, because the temperature difference might create air currents which move smoke away from the unit.

A requirement for maintenance can not be made as a condition of passing plans deposited with a Local Authority or Approved Inspector. However the attention of developers and builders is drawn to the desirability of providing the occupants with information on the use of the equipment, and on its maintenance (or guidance on suitable maintenance contractors).

Note that BS 5839: Part 1 recommends that occupiers should receive the manufacturers' instructions concerning the operation and maintenance of the alarm system.

Inner rooms
1.16 A room whose only escape route is through another room is at risk if a fire starts in that other room. It is termed an inner room and is at risk from a fire in the outer room (access room). This situation may arise with open plan layouts.

Such an arrangement is only acceptable where the inner room is:

a. a kitchen,

b. a laundry or utility room,

c. a dressing room,

d. a bathroom, wc, or shower room, or

e. any other room on the basement, ground or first storey, which has an openable window or external door suitable for escape or rescue, and which complies with paragraph 1.18.

Basements
1.17 Because combustion products tend to rise, there is a danger that people escaping from a fire in a basement would find that they had to move into a layer of smoke if they had to use an internal stair. Therefore if the basement storey contains a bedroom or an inner room which is a habitable room, there should be an alternative escape route from the basement via a door or window that is suitable for escape (see paragraph 1.18). If basement accommodation is not separated from the rest of the house (which is acceptable in a house with no storey more than 4.5m above ground level), the rooms on the other storeys are effectively inner rooms and are subject to the provisions of 1.16.

Windows and external doors for escape
1.18 Any window or external door provided for escape purposes should comply with the following conditions:

a. it should have an unobstructed opening that is at least 850mm high and 500mm wide, and the bottom of a window opening should be not more than 1100mm and not less than 800mm above the floor, except in the case of a roof window where the bottom of the opening may be 600mm above the floor (see Diagram 4);

b. it should enable the person escaping to reach a place free from danger from fire. This is a matter for judgement in each case, but in general a courtyard or back garden from which there is no exit other than through other buildings would have to be at least as deep as the dwelling is high to be acceptable, see Diagram 1.

c. where provided for escape from a room above ground storey level, a dormer window or roof window should be positioned in accordance with Diagram 4.

Balconies and flat roofs
1.19 Where a balcony or flat roof is provided for escape purposes guarding may be needed, in which case it should meet the provisions in Approved Document K, Stairs, ramps and guards.

Additional provisions for houses with a floor more than 4.5m above ground level

Houses with one storey having a floor more than 4.5 m above ground level

1.20 The house may either have a protected stairway as described in (a) below, or the top floor can be separated and given its own alternative escape route as described in (b). A variation of (b) can be used where the roofspace of an existing two storey dwelling house is being converted into habitable accommodation to form a three storey dwellinghouse, see paragraph 1.23-1.31.

a. The upper storeys (those above ground storey) should be served by a protected stairway which should either:

i. extend to a final exit see Diagram 2:(a), or

ii. give access to at least two escape routes at ground level, each delivering to final exits and separated from each other by fire-resisting construction and self-closing fire doors see Diagram 2:(b).

b. The top storey should be separated from the lower storeys by fire-resisting construction and be provided with an alternative escape route leading to its own final exit.

Houses with more than one floor over 4.5 m above ground level

1.21 Where a house has two or more storeys with floors more than 4.5m above ground level (typically a house of four or more storeys), some measures in addition to those in paragraph 1.20 may be needed. The guidance in clause 4.4 of BS 5588 *Fire precautions in the design and construction of buildings: Part 1 1990 Code of practice for residential buildings,* should be followed in such cases.

Ducted warm air heating systems in houses with a floor more than 4.5m above ground level

1.22 With this form of heating, precautions may be needed against the possibility of the system allowing smoke or fire to spread into a protected stairway. Guidance is set out in clause 6 of BS 5588: Part 1.

Diagram 2 Alternative arrangements for final exits

see para 1.20a & 1.24

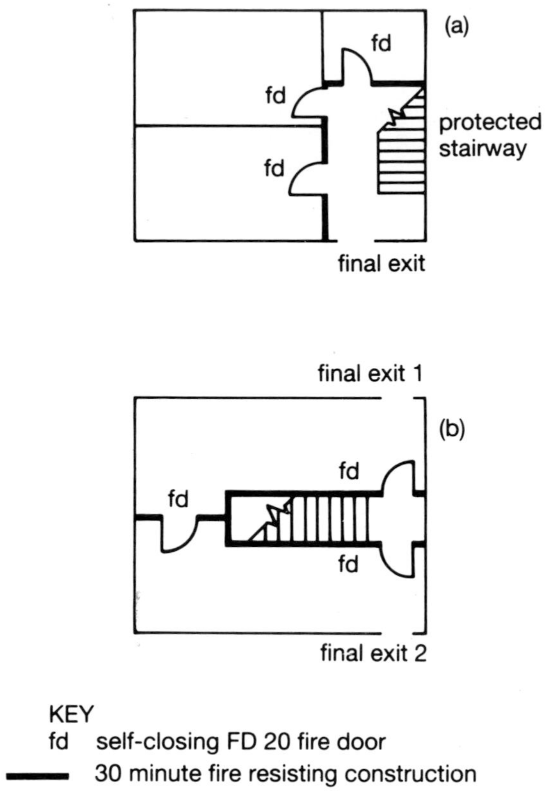

KEY
fd   self-closing FD 20 fire door
——   30 minute fire resisting construction

Loft conversions

1.23 In the case of an existing two storey dwelling house to which a storey is to be added by converting the existing roof space into habitable rooms the following provisions can be applied as an alternative to those in paragraph 1.20. However, these alternative provisions are not suitable if:-

a. the work involves raising the roofline above the existing ridge level, or

b. the new second storey exceeds 50m² in floor area, or

c. the new second storey is to contain more than two habitable rooms.

Enclosure of existing stair
1.24 The stair in the ground and first storeys should be enclosed with walls and/or partitions which are fire-resisting, and the enclosure should either:

a. extend to a final exit see Diagram 2:(a); or

b. give access to at least two escape routes at ground level, each delivering to final exits and separated from each other by fire-resisting construction and self-closing fire doors see Diagram 2:(b).

Doorways
1.25 Every doorway within the enclosure to the existing stair should be fitted with a door which, in the case of doors to habitable rooms, should be fitted with a self-closing device.

Any new door to a habitable room should be a fire door, but existing doors need only be made self-closing.

Glazing
1.26 Any glazing in the enclosure to the existing stair, including all doors (whether or not they need to be fire doors), but excluding glazing to a bathroom or w.c., should be fire-resisting.

New stair
1.27 The new storey should be served by a stair (which may be an alternating tread stair) meeting the provisions in Approved Document K, Stairs, ramps and guards. The new stair may be located either in a continuation of the existing stairway, or in an enclosure that is separated from the existing stairway, and from ground and first floor accommodation, but which opens into the existing stairway at first floor level, see Diagram 3.

Fire separation of new storey
1.28 The new storey should be separated from the rest of the house by fire-resisting construction, see Section 7. To maintain this separation, measures should be taken to prevent smoke and fire in the stairway from entering the new storey.

This may be achieved by providing a self-closing fire door set in fire-resisting construction either at the top or the bottom of the new stair, depending on the layout of the new stairway, see Diagram 3.

Diagram 3 Alternatives for the fire separation of the stair and new storey in house conversion.

see para 1.27 and 1.28

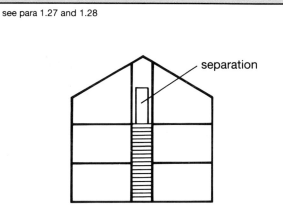

a. stair to new storey is within existing stairway. Separation of accommodation on new storey from stair is at top level.

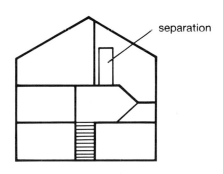

b. stair to new storey is in space converted and separated from first floor accommodation. New storey separated from stair at top level.

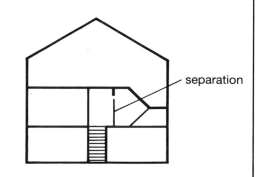

c. stair to new storey is in space converted and separated from first floor accommodation. New storey open to new stair. New stair separated from original stair at first floor level.

Escape windows

1.29 Windows provided for escape or rescue purposes from basement, ground or first storeys, provide a means of self-rescue. At higher level escape may depend on a ladder being set up. While this is a departure from the general principle that escape should be without outside assistance it is considered that, in the case of a three storey domestic residential loft conversion this is reasonable as an emergency measure.

1.30 The room (or rooms) in the new storey should each have an openable window or rooflight for escape or rescue purposes which meets the relevant provisions in Diagram 4. A door to a roof terrace is also acceptable. In a two room loft conversion, a single escape window can be accepted provided both rooms have their own access to the stairs. A communicating door between the rooms must be provided so that it is possible to gain access to the escape window without passing through the stair enclosure.

1.31 The window should be located to allow access for rescue by ladder from the ground (there should therefore be suitable pedestrian access to the point at which a ladder would be set, for fire service personnel to carry a ladder from their vehicle, although it should not be assumed that only the fire service will make a rescue).

Diagram 4 Position of dormer window or rooflight suitable for escape or rescue purposes from a loft conversion

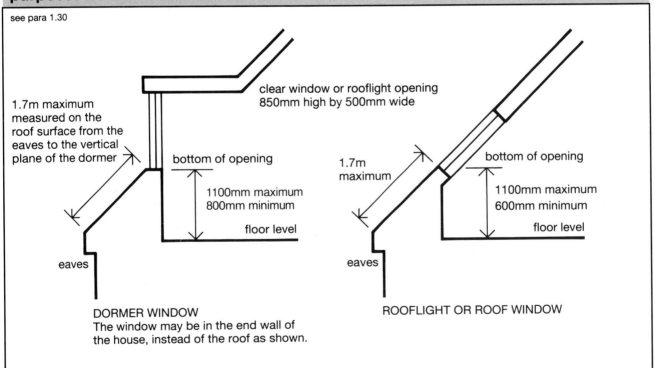

see para 1.30

1.7m maximum measured on the roof surface from the eaves to the vertical plane of the dormer

clear window or rooflight opening 850mm high by 500mm wide

bottom of opening

1100mm maximum
800mm minimum

floor level

eaves

DORMER WINDOW
The window may be in the end wall of the house, instead of the roof as shown.

1.7m maximum

bottom of opening

1100mm maximum
600mm minimum

floor level

eaves

ROOFLIGHT OR ROOF WINDOW

Section 2

FLATS AND MAISONETTES

Introduction

2.1 The means of escape from the basement, ground or first floor levels of a flat or maisonette are relatively simple to provide. Few provisions are specified in this section beyond ensuring that each habitable room either opens directly onto a hallway or stair leading to the entrance, or that it has a window or door through which escape could be made; and that means are provided for giving early warning in the event of fire. With increasing height more complex provisions are needed because escape through upper windows becomes increasingly hazardous, and in maisonettes internal stairs with a higher level of protection are needed.

2.2 The guidance in this section deals with some common arrangements of flat and maisonette design. Other, less common, arrangements (for example flats entered above or below accommodation level, or flats containing galleries) may also be acceptable. Guidance on these is given in clauses 9 and 10 of BS 5588: Part 1: 1990.

2.3 The provisions for means of escape for flats and maisonettes are based on the assumption that:

a. the fire is generally in a dwelling;

b. there is no reliance on external rescue (eg by a portable ladder);

c. measures in Section 8 (B3) provide a high degree of compartmentation and therefore a low probability of fire spread beyond the dwelling of origin, so that simultaneous evacuation of the building is unlikely to be necessary; and

d. although fires may occur in the common parts of the building, the materials and construction used there should prevent the fabric from being involved beyond the immediate vicinity (although in some cases communal facilities exist which require additional measures to be taken).

2.4 There are two distinct components to planning means of escape from buildings containing flats and maisonettes; escape from within each dwelling, and escape from each dwelling to the final exit from the building.

Paragraphs 2.7 to 2.17 deal with the means of escape within each unit, ie. within the private domestic area. Paragraphs 2.18 to 2.45 deal with the means of escape in the common areas of the building.

Houses in multiple occupation
2.5 This guidance is also applicable to flats and maisonettes which are considered to be houses in multiple occupation. A house in multiple occupation is defined in section 345 of the Housing Act 1985 as "a house which is occupied by persons who do not form a single household". Guidance on the interpretation of this wide-ranging definition is given in the joint Department of the Environment / Home Office / Welsh Office Circular (DoE 12/86; HO 39/86; WO 23/86) "Memorandum on overcrowding and houses in multiple occupation".

Sheltered housing
2.6 Whilst many of the provisions in this Approved Document for means of escape from flats are applicable to sheltered housing, the nature of the occupancy may necessitate some additional fire protection measures. The extent will depend on the form of the development. For example a group of specially adapted bungalows or 2 storey flats, with few communal facilities, need not be treated differently from other 1 or 2 storey houses or flats. Where additional provisions are needed guidance on means of escape can be found in clause 17 of BS 5588: Part 1: 1990.

Means of escape within flats and maisonettes

Automatic smoke detection and alarms
2.7 The installation of smoke detection and alarms can significantly increase the level of safety by automatically giving an early warning of fire. The guidance in 1.8-1.15 should be followed while noting that:

a. the provisions are not intended to be applied to the common parts of blocks of flats and do not include interconnection between installations in separate flats.

b. a flat with accommodation on more than one level (i.e. a maisonette) should be treated in the same way as a house with more than one storey.

Inner rooms
2.8 A room whose only escape route is through another room is at risk if a fire starts in that other room. The guidance in Section 1, paragraph 1.16, on inner rooms in dwellinghouses, applies equally to flats and maisonettes.

Basements
2.9 Because combustion products tend to rise, there is a danger that people escaping from a fire in a basement would find that they had to move into a layer of smoke if they had to use an internal stair. The guidance in Section 1 paragraph 1.17, about basements in dwellinghouses, applies equally to basement flats and maisonettes.

Balconies and flat roofs ·

2.10 The guidance in Section 1 paragraph 1.19 on balconies and flat roofs of dwellinghouses, applies equally to flats and maisonettes. In addition any balcony outside an alternative exit to a dwelling more than 4.5 m above ground level should be a common balcony and meet the conditions in paragraph 2.16.

Planning in flats where the floor is not more than 4.5m above ground level

2.11 No flat should be so planned that any habitable room is an inner room unless that room has an external door or window complying with Section 1 paragraph 1.18.

Additional provisions for flats and maisonettes with a floor more than 4.5 m above ground level

Internal planning of flats

2.12 Three acceptable approaches (all of which should observe the restrictions concerning inner rooms given in paragraph 2.8) when planning a flat which has a floor at more than 4.5 m above ground level are:

a. to provide a protected entrance hall which serves all habitable rooms, planned so that the travel distance from the entrance door to the door to any habitable room is 9 m or less (see Diagram 5), or

b. to plan the flat so that the travel distance from the entrance door to any point in any of the habitable rooms does not exceed 9 m and the cooking facilities are remote from the entrance door and do not prejudice the escape route from any point in the flat, (see Diagram 6), or

c. to provide an alternative exit from the flat, complying with paragraph 2.13.

see para 2.12a

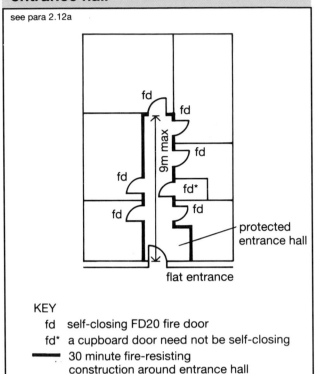

flat entrance

protected entrance hall

KEY
fd   self-closing FD20 fire door
fd*   a cupboard door need not be self-closing
———   30 minute fire-resisting construction around entrance hall

Diagram 6 **Flat with restricted travel distance from furthest point to entrance**

see para 2.12b

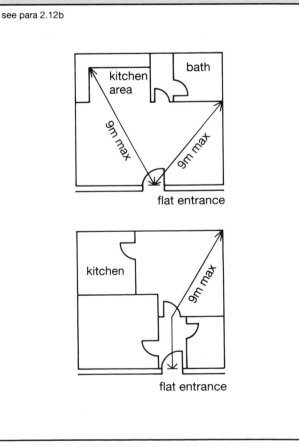

flat entrance

Diagram 7 Flat with an alternative exit, but where all habitable rooms have no direct access to an entrance hall

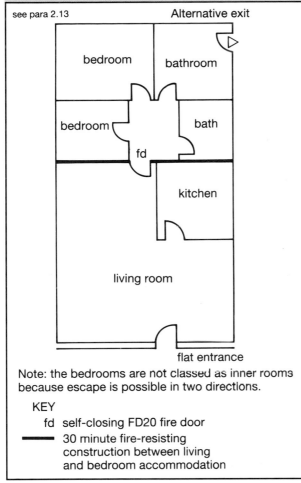

see para 2.13

Note: the bedrooms are not classed as inner rooms because escape is possible in two directions.

KEY
fd   self-closing FD20 fire door
━━ 30 minute fire-resisting construction between living and bedroom accommodation

2.13 Where any flat has an alternative exit and all habitable rooms do not have direct access to the entrance hall, (see Diagram 7):-

a. the bedrooms should be separated from the living accommodation by fire-resisting construction and self-closing fire-door(s), and

b. the alternative exit should be located in the part of the flat containing the bedroom(s).

Diagram 8 Maisonette with alternative exits from each habitable room except at entrance level

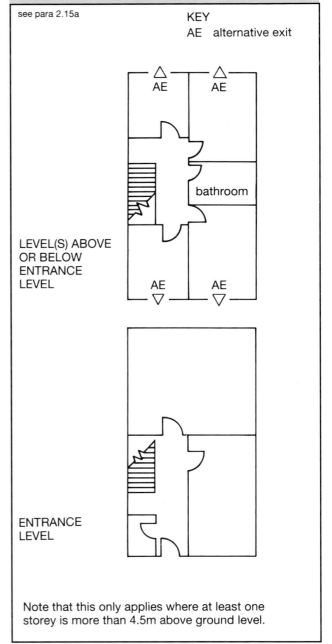

see para 2.15a

KEY
AE   alternative exit

Note that this only applies where at least one storey is more than 4.5m above ground level.

Internal planning of maisonettes

2.14 A maisonette with an independent external entrance at ground level is similar to a dwellinghouse and means of escape should be planned on the basis of paragraphs 1.20 or 1.21 depending on the height of the top storey above ground level.

2.15 Two acceptable approaches to planning a maisonette, which does not have its own external entrance at ground level but has a floor at more than 4.5m above ground level, are:

a.   To provide an alternative exit from each habitable room which is not on the entrance floor of the maisonette, see Diagram 8; or

b. To provide one alternative exit from each floor (other than the entrance floor), with a protected landing entered directly from all the habitable rooms on that floor, see Diagram 9.

Diagram 9 **Maisonette with protected entrance hall and landing**

see para 2.15b

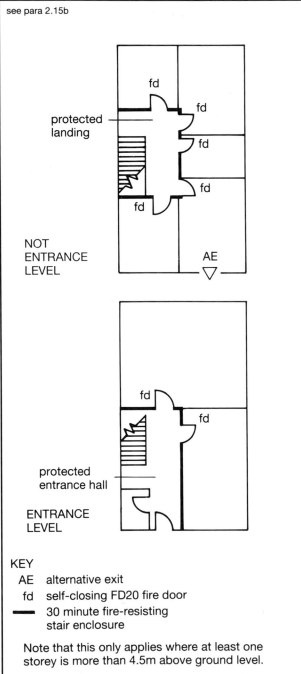

NOT
ENTRANCE
LEVEL

protected
landing

AE

protected
entrance hall

ENTRANCE
LEVEL

KEY

AE   alternative exit

fd   self-closing FD20 fire door

———   30 minute fire-resisting
stair enclosure

Note that this only applies where at least one storey is more than 4.5m above ground level.

Alternative exits

2.16 To be effective, an alternative exit from a flat or maisonette should satisfy the following conditions:

a. be remote from the main entrance door to the dwelling; and

b. lead to a final exit or common stair by way of

i. a door onto an access corridor or common balcony, or

ii. an internal private stair leading to an access corridor or common balcony at another level, or

iii. a door onto an external stair, or

iv. a door onto an escape route over a flat roof.

Ducted warm air heating systems in flats and maisonettes with a floor more than 4.5m above ground level

2.17 With this form of heating, precautions will be needed against the possibility of the system allowing smoke or fire to spread into a protected entrance hall or landing. Guidance is set out in clause 15 of BS 5588: Part 1:

Means of escape in the common parts of flats and maisonettes

The following paragraphs deal with means of escape from the entrance doors of dwellings, and from all other common parts of the building, to a final exit. They are not applicable where the top floor is not more than 4.5m above ground level. They should be read in conjunction with the general provisions in Section 5.

Number of escape routes

2.18 Every dwelling should have access to alternative escape routes so that a person confronted by the effects of an outbreak of fire in another dwelling can turn away from it and make a safe escape.

However, a single escape route from the dwelling entrance door is acceptable if either:

a.   the dwelling is situated in a storey served by a single common stair and:-

i.   every dwelling is separated from the common stair by a protected lobby or common corridor (see Diagream 10), and

ii   the travel distance limitations in Table 2, on escape in one direction only, are observed; or

b.   alternatively the dwelling is situated in a dead end part of a common corridor served by two (or more) common stairs, and the distance to the nearest common stair complies with the limitations in Table 2 on escape in one direction only (see Diagram 11).

Small single-stair buildings
2.19 The provisions in paragraph 2.18 may be modified and a single stair, protected in accordance with Diagram 12, may be used provided that:

a.   the top floor of the building is no more than 11m above ground level, and

b.   there are no more than 3 storeys above the ground level storey, and

c.   the stair does not connect to a covered car park, except if the car park is open-sided.

Flats and maisonettes with balcony or deck access
2.20 The provisions of paragraph 2.18 may also be modified in the case of flats and maisonettes with balcony or deck approach. Guidance on these forms of development is set out in clause 13 of BS 5588: Part 1: 1990.

Diagram 10 Flats or maisonettes served by one common stair

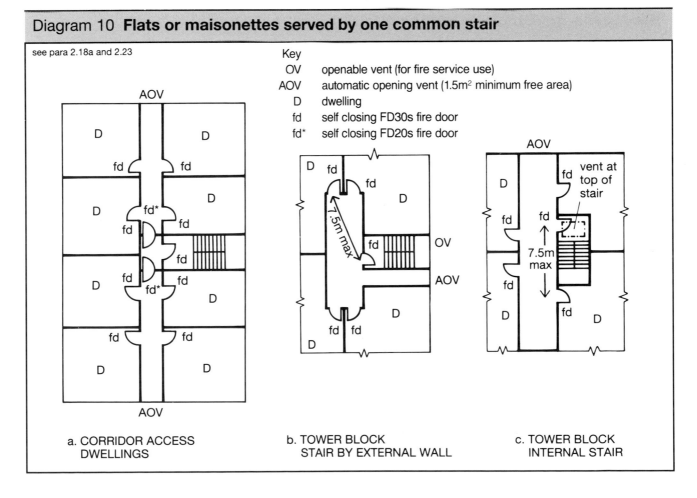

see para 2.18a and 2.23

Key
OV   openable vent (for fire service use)
AOV   automatic opening vent (1.5m^2 minimum free area)
D   dwelling
fd   self closing FD30s fire door
fd*   self closing FD20s fire door

a. CORRIDOR ACCESS DWELLINGS

b. TOWER BLOCK STAIR BY EXTERNAL WALL

c. TOWER BLOCK INTERNAL STAIR

B1

Diagram 11 Flats or maisonettes served by more than one common stair

see para 2.18b and 2.23

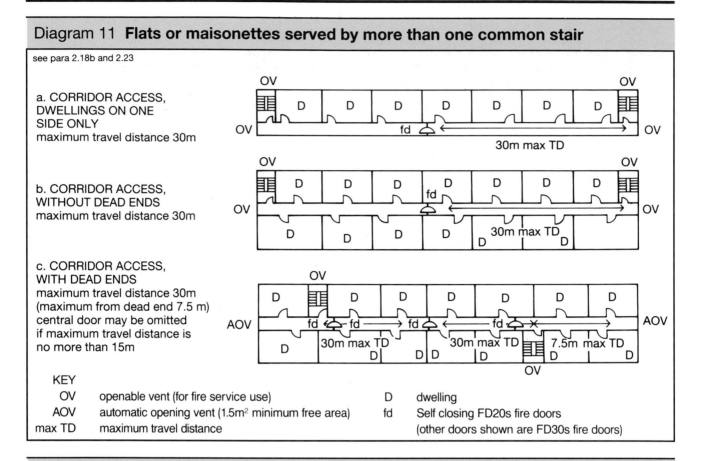

a. CORRIDOR ACCESS, DWELLINGS ON ONE SIDE ONLY
maximum travel distance 30m

b. CORRIDOR ACCESS, WITHOUT DEAD ENDS
maximum travel distance 30m

c. CORRIDOR ACCESS, WITH DEAD ENDS
maximum travel distance 30m
(maximum from dead end 7.5 m)
central door may be omitted if maximum travel distance is no more than 15m

KEY
OV	openable vent (for fire service use)	D	dwelling
AOV	automatic opening vent (1.5m² minimum free area)	fd	Self closing FD20s fire doors (other doors shown are FD30s fire doors)
max TD	maximum travel distance		

Diagram 12 Common escape route in small single stair building

see para 2.19

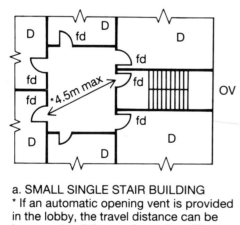

a. SMALL SINGLE STAIR BUILDING
* If an automatic opening vent is provided in the lobby, the travel distance can be increased to 7.5m maximum (see Diagram 10 example b).

b. SMALL SINGLE STAIR BUILDING WITH NO MORE THAN 2 DWELLINGS PER STOREY
The door between stair and lobby should be free from security fastenings.
If the dwellings have protected entrance halls, the lobby between the common stair and dwelling entrance is not essential.

KEY

———	fire-resisting construction
fd	self-closing FD30S fire door;
OV	openable vent for fire service use (it may be replaced by a vent over the stair).
D	dwelling

Common escape routes

Planning of common escape routes

2.21 Escape routes in the common areas should comply with the limitations on travel distance in Table 2. However there may be circumstances where some increase on these maximum figures will be reasonable.

Escape routes should be planned so that people do not have to pass through one stairway enclosure to reach another. However it is acceptable to pass through a protected lobby of one stairway in order to reach another.

Table 2 **Limitations on distance of travel in common areas of flat and maisonette buildings** (see paragraph 2.21)	
Maximum distance of travel (m) from dwelling entrance door to common stair, or to door to lobby in corridor-access single stair flats (Diagram 10a)	
Escape in one direction only	Escape in more than one direction
7.5 (1)(2)	30 (2)

1. Reduced to 4.5m in the case shown in diagram 12a.

2. Where all dwellings on a storey have independent alternative means of escape, the maximum distance of travel does not apply. However all parts of the building need to be within 60m of fire mains, refer to the guidance on B5, (Sections 15-18).

Protection of common escape routes

2.22 To reduce the risk of a fire in a dwelling affecting the means of escape from other dwellings, and common parts of the building, the common corridors should be protected corridors.

The wall between each dwelling and the corridor should be a compartment wall (see Section 8).

Ventilation of common escape routes

2.23 Despite the provisions described in this Approved Document, it is probable that some smoke will get into a common corridor or lobby from a fire in a dwelling, if only because the entrance door will be open when the occupants escape.

There should therefore be some means of ventilating the common escape routes to disperse smoke:

a. in single stair buildings, other than small ones complying with Diagram 12, and in any dead-end portion of a building with more than one stair, the common corridor or lobby should be ventilated by an automatic opening ventilator, triggered by automatic smoke detection located in the space to be ventilated. The ventilator should have a free area of at least 1.5m^2, and be fitted with a manual override. (See also Diagram 10 and Diagram 11c).

b. In buildings with more than one stair, common corridors should extend at both ends to the external face of the building where there should be openable ventilators, which may operate automatically, for fire service use (see Diagram 11a. and b.). The free area of the ventilators should be at least 1.5m^2 at each end of the corridor.

Sub-division of common escape routes

2.24 A common corridor that connects two or more storey exits should be sub-divided by a self-closing fire door with, if necessary, any associated fire-resisting screen (see Diagram 11). The door(s) should be positioned so that smoke will not affect access to more than one stairway.

2.25 A dead end portion of a common corridor should be separated from the rest of the corridor by a self-closing fire door with, if necessary, any associated fire-resisting screen (see Diagram 10a and Diagram 11c).

Pressurization of common escape routes

2.26 Where the escape stairway and corridors/lobbies are protected by a smoke control system employing pressure differentials complying with BS 5588: Part 4, the cross corridor fire doors and the openable and automatically opening vents should be omitted.

Ancillary accommodation, etc

2.27 Stores and other ancillary accommodation should not be located within, or entered from, any protected lobby or protected corridor forming part of a common escape route. However refer to paragraphs 5.47 to 5.50 for special provisions for refuse chutes and storage areas.

Escape routes over flat roofs

2.28 If more than one escape route is available from a storey, or part of a building, one of those routes may be by way of a flat roof, provided that:

a. the roof is part of the same building from which escape is being made;

b. the route across the roof leads to a storey exit;

c. the part of the roof forming the escape route and its supporting structure, together with any opening within 3m of the escape route, is fire-resisting (see Appendix A Table A1); and

d. the route is adequately defined and guarded by walls and/or protective barriers which meet the provisions in Approved Document K, Stairs, ramps and guards.

Common stairs

Number of common stairs

2.29 As explained in paragraph 2.18 and paragraph 2.19 a single common stair can be acceptable in some cases, but otherwise there should be access to more than one common stair for escape purposes.

Width of common stairs

2.30 The minimum width of a common stair should be 1 m unless it is also a firefighting stair, when it should be at least 1.1 m wide. (see paragraph 0.40 for measurement of width).

Protection of common stairs

General

2.31 Common stairs need to have a satisfactory standard of fire protection if they are to fulfil their role as areas of relative safety during a fire evacuation. The provisions in paragraphs 2.32 to 2.45 below should be followed.

2.32 Stairs provide a potential route for fire spread from floor to floor. In Section 8 under the requirement of B3 to inhibit internal fire spread, there is guidance on the enclosure of stairs to avoid this. A stair may also serve as a fire fighting stair in accordance with the requirement B5, in which case account will have to be taken of guidance in Section 17.

Enclosure of common stairs

2.33 Every common stair should be situated within a fire-resisting enclosure (ie it should be a protected stair), to reduce the risk of smoke and heat making use of the stair hazardous.

2.34 The appropriate level of fire resistance is given in Appendix A Tables A1 and A2

Exits from protected stairways

2.35 Every protected stairway should discharge:

a. directly to a final exit; or

b. by way of a protected exit passageway to a final exit.

Separation of adjoining protected stairways

2.36 Where two protected stairways (or exit passageways leading to different final exits) are adjacent, they should be separated by an imperforate enclosure.

Use of space within protected stairways

2.37 A protected stairway needs to be relatively free of potential sources of fire. Consequently, it should not be used for anything else, except a lift well. There are other provisions for lifts in paragraphs 5.37 to 5.42.

Fire resistance and openings in external walls of protected stairways

2.38 With some configurations of external wall, a fire in one part of a building could subject the external wall of a protected stairway to heat (for example, where the two are adjacent at an internal angle in the facade as shown in Diagram 13). If the external wall of the protected stairway has little fire resistance, there is a risk that this could prevent the safe use of the stair. Therefore, if:

a. a protected stairway projects beyond, or is recessed from, or is in an internal angle of, the adjoining external wall of the building, then

b. the distance between any unprotected area in the external enclosures to the building and any unprotected area in the enclosure to the stairway should be at least 1.8m (see Diagram 13).

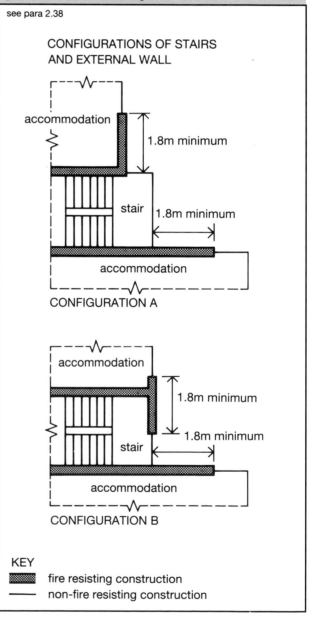

Diagram 13 External protection to protected stairways

see para 2.38

CONFIGURATIONS OF STAIRS AND EXTERNAL WALL

accommodation

1.8m minimum

stair

1.8m minimum

accommodation

CONFIGURATION A

accommodation

1.8m minimum

1.8m minimum

stair

accommodation

CONFIGURATION B

KEY

▨ fire resisting construction

— non-fire resisting construction

Gas service pipes in protected stairways

2.39 Gas service pipes or associated meters should not be incorporated within a protected stairway unless the gas installation is in accordance with the requirements for installation and connection set out in the Gas Safety Regulations 1972 (SI. 1972/1178) and the Gas Safety (Installation and Use) Regulations 1984 (SI. 1984/1358) as amended by the Gas Safety (Installation and use) (Amendment) Regulations 1990.

Basement stairs

2.40 Because of their situation, basement stairways are more likely to be filled with smoke and heat than stairs in ground and upper storeys.

Special measures are therefore needed in order to prevent a basement fire endangering upper storeys. These are set out in the following two paragraphs.

2.41 If an escape stair forms part of the only escape route from an upper storey of a building (or part of a building) it should not be continued down to serve any basement storey. The basement should be served by a separate stair.

2.42 If there is more than one escape stair from an upper storey of a building (or part of a building), only one of the stairs serving the upper storeys of the building (or part) need be terminated at ground level. Other stairs may connect with the basement storey(s) if there is a ventilated protected lobby, or a ventilated protected corridor between the stair(s) and accommodation at each basement level.

Stairs serving accommodation ancillary to flats and maisonettes

2.43 Where a common stair forms part of the only escape route from a dwelling, it should not also serve any covered car park, boiler room, fuel storage space or other ancillary accommodation of similar fire risk.

2.44 Any common stair which does not form part of the only escape route from a dwelling may also serve ancillary accommodation if it is separated from the ancillary accommodation by a protected lobby.

External escape stairs

2.45 If more than one escape route is available from a storey (or part of a building), one of the escape routes from that storey or part of the building may be by way of an external escape stair if it meets the following provisions:

a. The stair serves a floor not more than 6 m above either the ground level or a roof or podium which is itself served by an independent protected stairway (see Diagram 14b).

b. All doors giving access to the stair should be fire-resisting and self-closing, except that a fire-resisting door is not required at the head of any stair leading downwards where there is only one exit from the building onto the top landing.

c. Any part of the external walls within 1.8 m of (and 9m vertically below), the flights and landings of an external escape stair should be of fire-resisting construction, except that the 1.8m dimension may be reduced to 1.1m above the top level of the stair if it is not a stair up from a basement to ground level (see Diagram 14).

d. There is protection by fire-resisting construction for any part of the building (including any doors) within 3m of the escape route from the stair to a place of safety.

Flats in mixed use buildings

2.46 In buildings with not more than 3 storeys above the ground storey, stairs may serve both dwellings and non-residential occupancies, provided that the stairs are separated from each occupancy by protected lobbies at all levels.

2.47 In buildings with more than three storeys above the ground storey:

a. all stairs serving flats should not communicate with any other part of the building, unless the flat is ancillary to the main use of the building;

b. if the flat is ancillary to the main use of the building a stair serving the flat may serve other parts of the building provided that:

i. the stair is separated from any such parts on lower storeys by protected lobbies (at those storey levels); and

ii. an independent alternative escape route is provided from the flat; and

iii. any automatic fire detection and alarm system with which the main part of the building is fitted also covers the flat.

Diagram 14 Fire resistance of areas adjacent to external stairs

see para 2.45

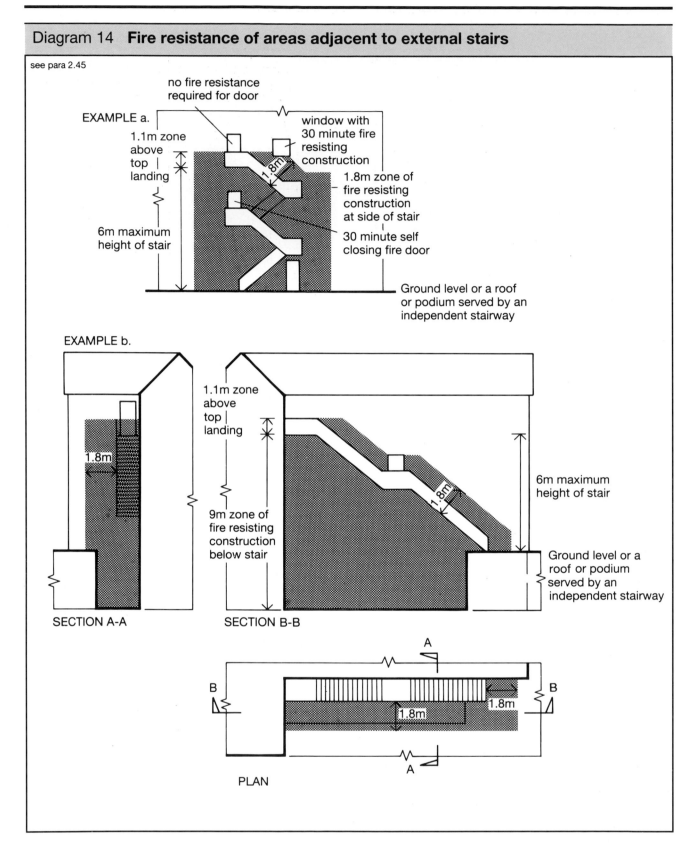

EXAMPLE a.

no fire resistance required for door

1.1m zone above top landing

6m maximum height of stair

window with 30 minute fire resisting construction

1.8m zone of fire resisting construction at side of stair

30 minute self closing fire door

Ground level or a roof or podium served by an independent stairway

EXAMPLE b.

1.1m zone above top landing

1.8m

9m zone of fire resisting construction below stair

6m maximum height of stair

Ground level or a roof or podium served by an independent stairway

SECTION A-A

SECTION B-B

1.8m

PLAN

Section 3

DESIGN FOR HORIZONTAL ESCAPE - BUILDINGS OTHER THAN DWELLINGS

Introduction

3.1 The general principle to be followed when designing facilities for means of escape is that any person confronted by an outbreak of fire within a building can turn away from it and make a safe escape. This Section deals with the provision of means of escape from any point to the storey exit of the floor in question, for all types of building other than dwelling houses, flats and maisonettes (for which refer to Sections 1 & 2).

This Section should be read in conjunction with the guidance on the vertical part of the escape route in Section 4 and the general provisions in Section 5.

Escape route design

Number of escape routes and exits

3.2 The number of escape routes and exits to be provided depends on the number of occupants in the room, tier or storey in question, and the limits on travel distance to the nearest exit given in Table 3.

3.3 In multi-storey buildings (see Section 4) more than one stair may be needed for escape, in which case every part of each storey will need to have access to more than one stair. This does not prevent areas from being in a dead end condition provided that the alternative stair is accessible in case the first one is not usable.

3.4 If a building contains a mixture of purpose groups the means of escape from any part in a residential (purpose groups 1 or 2) or assembly and recreation (purpose group 5) purpose group should be independent from the means of escape serving other parts. (See paragraphs 2.46 and 2.47 for guidance on flats, and Appendix D for definitions of purpose groups).

Single escape routes and exits

3.5 In order to avoid occupants being trapped by fire or smoke, there should be alternative escape routes from all parts of the building. However in the following situations a single route is acceptable:

a. areas from which a storey exit can be reached within the travel distance limit for travel in one direction set in Table 3, provided that no one room in this situation has an occupant capacity of more than 50 people, or 30 people if the building is in Institutional use (Purpose Group 2a). The calculation of capacity is described in 0.38;

b. a storey (except one used for in-patient care in a hospital) with an occupant capacity of not more than 50 people, where the limits on travel in one direction only are satisfied (see Table 3).

3.6 In many cases there will not be an alternative at the beginning of the route. For example, there may be only one exit from a room to a corridor, from which point escape is possible in two directions. This is acceptable provided that the overall distance to the nearest storey exit is within the limits for routes where there is an alternative, and the 'one direction only' section of the route does not exceed the limit for travel where there is no alternative, see Table 3, and Diagram 15.

Diagram 15 Travel distance in dead end condition

see para 3.6

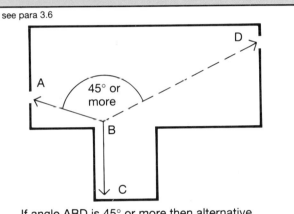

If angle ABD is 45° or more then alternative routes are available from point B, so that CA or CD (whichever is the less) should be no more than the maximum distance of travel given for alternative routes, and CB should be no more than the maximum distance for travel where there are no alternative routes.

Table 3 Limitations on travel distance

Purpose Group	Use of the premises or part of the premises	Maximum travel distance(1) where travel is possible in:	
		one direction only (m)	more than one direction (m)
2(a)	Institutional (2)	9	18
2(b)	Other residential:		
	(a) in bedrooms (3)	9	18
	(b) in bedroom corridors	9	35
	(c) elsewhere	18	35
3	Office	18	45
4	Shop and Commercial (4)	18	45
5	Assembly and Recreation:		
	(a) buildings primarily for the handicapped except schools	9	18
	(b) elsewhere	15	32
6	Industrial (5)	25	45
7	Storage and other non-residential (5)	18	45
2-7	Place of special fire risk (6)	9(3)	18(3)
2-7	Plant room or rooftop plant:		
	(a) distance within the room	9	35
	(b) escape route not in open air (overall travel distance)	18	45
	(c) escape route in open air (overall travel distance)	60	100

Notes:

1. The dimensions in the Table are travel distances. If the internal layout of partitions, fittings, etc. is not known when plans are deposited, direct distances may be used for assessment. The direct distance is taken as 2/3rds. of the travel distance.

2. If provision for means of escape is being made in a hospital or other health care building by following the detailed guidance in the relevant part of the Department of Health "Firecode", the recommendations about travel distances in the appropriate "Firecode" document should be followed.

3. Maximum part of travel distance within the room.

4. Maximum travel distances within shopping malls are given in BS 5588: Part 10: 1991. Guidance on associated smoke control measures is given in a BRE report *Design principles for smoke ventilation in enclosed shopping centres BR 186.*

5. In industrial buildings the appropriate travel distance depends on the level of fire risk associated with the processes and materials being used. Control over the use of industrial buildings is exercised through the Fire Precautions Act. Attention is drawn to the guidance issued by the Home Office *Guide to fire precautions in existing places of work that require a fire certificate Factories Offices Shops and Railway Premises.* The dimensions given above assume that the premises will be of "normal" fire risk, as described in the Home Office guidance. If the building is high risk, as assessed against the criteria in the Home Office guidance, then lesser distances of 12m in one direction and 25m in more than one direction, would apply.

6. Places of special fire risk are listed in the definitions in Appendix E.

Diagram 16 Alternative escape routes

see para 3.8a

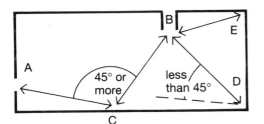

Alternative routes are available from C because angle ACB is 45° or more, so that either CA or CB should be less than the maximum travel distance given in Table 3.

Alternative routes are not available from D because angle ADB is less than 45° so that DB should not exceed the distance for travel in one direction (see Table 3). There is also no alternative route from E.

Alternative escape routes

3.8 A choice of escape routes is of little value if they are all likely to be disabled simultaneously. Alternative escape routes should therefore satisfy the following criteria:

a. they are in directions 45° or more apart (see Diagram 16); or

b. they are in directions less than 45° apart, but are separated from each other by fire-resisting construction.

Number of occupants and exits

3.7 The figure used for the number of occupants will normally be that specified as the basis for the design. When the number of occupants likely to use a room, tier or storey is not known, the capacity should be calculated on the basis of the appropriate floor space factors. Guidance for this is set out in paragraph 0.38 and Table 1.

Table 4 gives the minimum number of escape routes and exits from a room, tier or storey according to the number of occupants. (This number is likely to be increased by the need to observe travel distances, and by other practical considerations.).

The width of escape routes and exits is the subject of paragraph 3.15.

Table 4 Minimum number of escape routes and exits from a room, tier or storey

Maximum number of persons	Minimum number of escape routes/exits
500	2 (1)
1000	3
2000	4
4000	5
7000	6
11000	7
16000	8
more than 16000	8 (2)

Notes:

1. See paragraph 3.5 about the circumstances in which single exits and escape routes are acceptable.
2. Plus 1 per 5000 persons (or part thereof) over 16000.

Inner rooms

3.9 A room from which the only escape route is through another room is called an inner room. It is at risk if a fire starts in the other room, called the access room.

Such an arrangement is only acceptable if the following conditions are satisfied:

a. The occupant capacity of the inner room should not exceed 50 (30 in the case of a building in purpose group 2a (Institutional));

b. The inner room should not be a bedroom;

c. The escape route from the inner room should not pass through more than one access room;

d. The travel distance from any point in the inner room to the exit(s) from the access room should not exceed the appropriate limit given in Table 3.

e. The access room should not be a place of special fire risk and should be in the control of the same occupier; and

f. One of the following arrangements should be made:

i. the enclosures (walls or partitions) of the inner room should be stopped at least 500mm below the ceiling, or

ii. a vision panel which need not be more than 0.1m² should be located in the door or walls of the inner room, to enable occupants of the inner room to see if a fire has started in the outer room, or

iii. the access room should be fitted with a suitable automatic fire detection and alarm system to warn the occupants of the inner room of the outbreak of a fire in the access room.

Planning of exits in a central core

3.10 Buildings with more than one exit in a central core should be planned so that storey exits are remote from one another, and so that no two exits are approached from the same lift hall, common lobby or undivided corridor, or linked by any of these. (See Diagram 17).

Access to storey exits

3.11 Any storey which has more than one escape stair, should be planned so that it is not necessary to pass through one stairway to reach another. However it would be acceptable to pass through one stairway's protected lobby to reach another stair.

Separation of circulation routes from stair-ways

3.12 A protected stairway should not form part of the primary circulation route between different parts of the building at the same level. This is because the self-closing fire doors are more likely to be rendered ineffective as a result of their constant use, or because some occupants may regard them as an impediment. For example the doors are likely to be wedged open or have their closers removed.

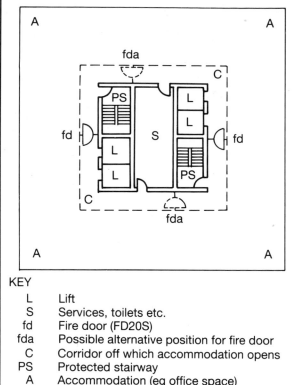

Diagram 17 Exits in a central core
see para 3.10

KEY

L	Lift
S	Services, toilets etc.
fd	Fire door (FD20S)
fda	Possible alternative position for fire door
C	Corridor off which accommodation opens
PS	Protected stairway
A	Accommodation (eg office space)

Storeys divided into different occupancies

3.13 Where any storey is divided into separate occupancies (ie where there are separate ownerships or tenancies of different organisations):

a. the means of escape from each occupancy should not pass through any other occupancy; and

b. if the means of escape include a common corridor or circulation space then either it should be a protected corridor or a suitable automatic fire detection and alarm system should be installed throughout the storey. See also paragraph 8.10 on compartmentation

Height of escape routes

3.14 All escape routes should have a clear headroom of not less than 2m except in doorways.

Width of escape routes and exits

3.15 The width of escape routes and exits depends on the number of persons needing to use them. They should not be less than the dimensions given in Table 5.

Table 5 Widths of escape routes and exits (1)

Maximum number of persons	Minimum width mm(2)
50	800 (3)
110	900
220	1100
more than 220	5 per person

Notes:

1. Refer to paragraph 0.40 on methods of measurement of width.

2. Refer to the guidance in the Approved Document to part M on minimum widths for areas accessible to disabled people.

3. May be reduced to 530mm for gangways between fixed storage racking, other than in public areas of Purpose Group 4 (shop and commercial).

3.16 Where the maximum number of people likely to use the escape route and exit is not known, the appropriate capacity should be calculated on the basis of the occupant capacity. Guidance is set out in paragraph 0.38 and Table 1.

3.17 If a storey has two or more storey exits it has to be assumed that a fire might prevent the occupants from using one of them. The remaining exit(s) need to be wide enough to allow all the occupants leave quickly. Therefore when deciding on the total width of exits needed according to Table 5, the largest exit should be discounted. This may have implications for the width of stairways,

because they should be at least as wide as any storey exit leading onto them. Although some stairways are not subject to discounting (see paragraph 4.11) storey exits onto them will be.

3.18 Guidance on the spacing of fixed seating for auditoria and the like, is given in BS 5588: Part 6: *Code of practice for assembly buildings.*

Protected corridors

3.19 A corridor which serves a part of the means of escape in any of the following circumstances should be a protected corridor:

a. every corridor within residential accommodation;

b. every dead-end corridor; and

c. any corridor common to two or more different occupancies (see also paragraph 3.13)

Enclosure of corridors that are not protected corridors

3.20 Where a corridor that is used as a means of escape, but is not a protected corridor, is enclosed by partitions, those partitions provide some defence against the spread of smoke in the early stages of a fire, even though they may have no fire resistance rating. To maintain this defence the partitions should be carried up to the soffit of the structural floor above, or to a suspended ceiling, and openings into rooms from the corridor should be fitted with doors, which need not be fire doors. Open planning, while offering no impediment to smoke spread, has the compensation that occupants can become aware of a fire quickly.

Diagram 18 Dead-end corridors

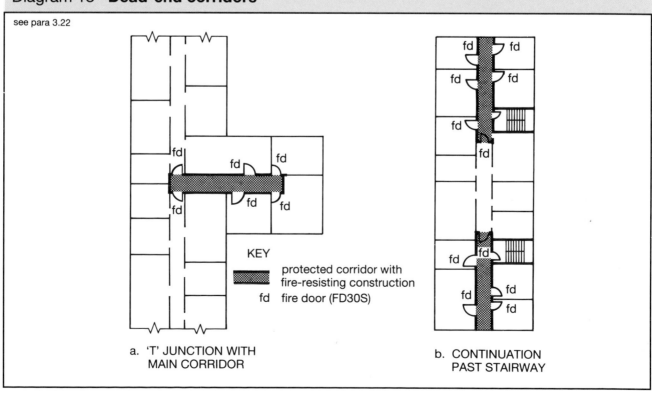

see para 3.22

KEY

▓▓ protected corridor with fire-resisting construction

fd fire door (FD30S)

a. 'T' JUNCTION WITH MAIN CORRIDOR

b. CONTINUATION PAST STAIRWAY

Sub-division of corridors

3.21 If a corridor provides access to alternative escape routes, there is a risk that smoke will spread along it and make both routes impassable before all occupants have escaped.

To avoid this, every corridor more than 12m long which connects two or more storey exits, should be sub-divided by self-closing fire doors (and any necessary associated screens) so that:

a. no length of undivided corridor is common to two storey exits; and

b. the fire door(s) are positioned to protect the route from smoke, having regard to the layout of the corridor and to any adjacent fire risks.

3.22 If a dead-end portion of a corridor provides access to a point from which alternative escape routes are available, there is a risk that smoke from a fire could make both routes impassable before the occupants in the dead-end have escaped. To avoid this, unless the escape stairway(s) and corridors are protected by a pressurization system complying with BS 5588: Part 4, every dead end corridor exceeding 4.5m in length should be separated by self-closing fire doors (together with any necessary associated screens) from any part of the corridor which:

a. provides two directions of escape (see Diagram 18:(a)) or

b. continues past one storey exit to another (see Diagram 18:(b))

External escape routes

3.23 Guidance on the use of external escape stairs from buildings other than dwellings is given in paragraph 4.35.

3.24 Where an external escape route other than a stair is beside an external wall of the building, that part of the external wall within 3m of the escape route should be of fire-resisting construction, up to a height of 1.1m above the paving level of the route.

Escape over flat roofs

3.25 If more than one escape route is available from a storey, or part of a building, one of those routes may be by way of a flat roof, provided that:

a. the route does not serve an Institutional building, or part of a building intended for use by members of the public;

b. the roof is part of the same building from which escape is being made;

c. the route across the roof leads to a storey exit;

d. the part of the roof forming the escape route and its supporting structure, together with any opening within 3 m of the escape route, is fire-resisting (see Appendix A Table A1); and

e. the route is adequately defined and guarded by walls and/or protective barriers which meet the provisions in Approved Document K, Stairs, ramps and guards

Hospitals and other residential care premises of Purpose Group 2a

General

3.26 Paragraph 0.34 explains that the Department of Health "Firecode" documents should be used in the design of health care and other institutional premises, where the normal principles of evacuation are inappropriate. The guidance referred to in 0.34 may be used for non-NHS premises.

3.27 One of the features of that guidance is the concept of progressive horizontal evacuation. This allows progressive horizontal escape to be made by evacuating into adjoining compartments, or sub-divisions of compartments, in those areas used for in-patient care. The object is to provide a place of relative safety within a short distance, from which further evacuation can be made if necessary but under less pressure of time.

Diagram 19 **Progressive horizontal evacuation**

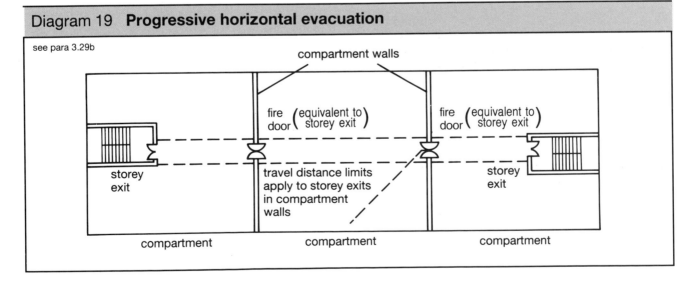

Planning for progressive horizontal evacuation

3.28 The adoption of progressive horizontal evacuation may be of value in some other residential buildings. The following guidance is given for buildings to which the provisions of the "Firecode" documents are not applicable.

3.29 In planning a storey which is divided into compartments for progressive horizontal evacuation, the following conditions should be observed:

a. Adjoining compartments into which horizontal evacuation may take place should each have a floor area sufficient to accommodate not only their own occupants but also the occupants from the adjoining compartment. This should be calculated on the basis of the design occupancy of the compartments.

b. Each compartment should have at least one other escape route, independent of the route into the adjoining compartment, see Diagram 19. This other route may be by way of a third compartment, provided the exit from that compartment is independent of the exits from the other compartments.

Compartmentation

3.30 Every upper storey used for in-patient care should be divided into at least two compartments in such a way as to permit progressive horizontal evacuation of each compartment.

Assembly buildings

3.31 There are particular problems that arise when people are limited in their ability to escape by fixed seating. This may occur at sports events, theatres, lecture halls and conference centres etc. Guidance on this and other aspects of means of escape in assembly buildings is given in sections 3 and 5 of BS 5588: Part 6: and the relevant recommendations of that code should be followed, in appropriate cases.

In the case of buildings to which the Safety of Sports Grounds Act 1975 applies, the guidance in the *Guide to safety at sports grounds* (HMSO) should be followed.

Schools and other education buildings

3.32 The design of the means of escape in school and other education buildings in purpose group 5, should be in accordance with the Department of Education and Science Building Bulletin 7, *Fire and the design of educational buildings* (HMSO 1988).

3.33 Provisions for means of escape in certain specialised buildings found on some school or other education premises, but outside the scope of Building Bulletin 7, should be made by reference to British Standards or other guidance referred to here for that building type.

Shops

3.34 An alternative approach to the provision of means of escape in shops is available in BS 5588: Part 2: *Code of practice for shops*. If that approach is adopted all the relevant provisions of that code should be followed (section 2,3,4 and 5) rather than a mixture of the code and provisions of sections 3-5 of this Approved Document.

In the case of small shops (ones with no storey larger than 280m^2, and having no more than 2 storeys plus a basement storey), the guidance in clause 9 of BS 5588: Part 2, may be followed instead of the provisions in this section. Note that BS 5588: Part 10 (shopping complexes) applies more restrictive provisions to units with only one exit.

Shopping complexes

3.35 Although the guidance in this Approved Document may be readily applied to individual shops, shopping complexes present a different set of escape problems. Guidance on means of escape in shopping complexes is given in section 4 of BS 5588: Part 10: *Code of practice for enclosed shopping complexes*.

Offices

3.36 An alternative approach to the provision of means of escape in office buildings is available in BS 5588: Part 3: *Code of practice for office buildings*. If that approach is adopted all the relevant provisions of that code should be followed (sections 2,3,4 and 5) rather than a mixture of the code and provisions of sections 3-5 of this Approved Document.

Section 4

DESIGN FOR VERTICAL ESCAPE - BUILDINGS OTHER THAN DWELLINGS

Introduction

4.1 An important aspect of means of escape in multi-storey buildings is the availability of a sufficient number of adequately sized and protected escape stairs. This Section deals with escape stairs and includes measures necessary to protect them in all types of building other than dwellinghouses, flats and maisonettes (for which see Sections 1 & 2).

This Section should be read in conjunction with the general provisions in Section 5.

Number of escape stairs

4.2 The number of escape stairs needed in a building (or part of a building) will be determined by:

a. the constraints imposed in Section 3 on the design of horizontal escape routes;

b. whether independent stairs are required in mixed occupancy buildings (see paragraph 4.4);

c. whether a single stair is acceptable (see paragraph 4.5); and

d. provision of adequate width for escape (see paragraph 4.6) while allowing for the possibility that a stair may have to be discounted because of fire or smoke (see paragraph 4.11).

4.3 In larger buildings, provisions for access for the fire service may apply in which case some escape stairs may also need to serve as firefighting stairs. The number of escape stairs may therefore be affected by provisions made in Section 17, paras 17.7 and 17.8.

4.4 Where a building contains storeys (or parts of storeys) in different purpose groups, if one of those purpose groups is either assembly and recreation or residential it should have means of escape independent from the means of escape serving any other purpose group (see also paragraphs 2.46 and 2.47).

Single escape stairs

4.5 Provided that independent escape routes are not necessary from areas in different purpose groups, in accordance with paragraph 4.4, the situations where a building (or part of a building) may be served by a single escape stair are:

a. from a basement which is allowed to have a single escape route in accordance with paragraph 3.5b

b. from a building which has no storey with a floor level more than 11m above ground level, and in which every storey is allowed to have a single escape route in accordance with paragraph 3.5b

c. in the case of offices, in situations where the recommendations of clause 8 of BS 5588: Part 3: 1983 *Code of practice for office buildings,* are followed.

Width of escape stairs

4.6 The width of escape stairs should:

a. be not less than the width(s) required for any exit(s) affording access to them;

b. conform with the minimum widths given in Table 6:

Table 6 Minimum width of escape stairs

Situation of stair	Max number of people served(1)	Minimum stair width (mm)
1. In an institutional building (unless the stair will only be used by staff)	150	1000
2. In an assembly building and serving an area used for assembly purposes (unless the area is less than 100m²)	220	1100
3. In any other building and serving an area with an occupancy of more than 50	over 220	note(2)
4. Any stair not described above	50	800

Notes:

1. Assessed as likely to use the stair in a fire emergency.
2. See Table 7 for sizing stairs for total evacuation, and Table 8 for phased evacuation.

c. not exceed 1400mm if their vertical extent is more than 30m, unless it is at least 1800mm and is provided with a central handrail (see note below) ;

d. not reduce in width at any point on the way to a final exit.

Note: The 1400mm width has been given for stairs in tall buildings because research indicates that people prefer to stay within reach of a handrail, when making a prolonged descent, so that the centre part of a wider stair is little used and could be hazardous. Thus additional stair(s) may be needed. Buildings with a floor more than 30m above ground level may also be designed on the basis of phased evacuation if the provisions in paragraph 4.19 are met.

4.7 If the resultant width of the stair is more than 1800mm, then for reasons of safety in use the stair should have a central handrail. In such a case the stair width on each side of the central handrail needs to be considered separately for the purpose of assessing stair capacity.

4.8 Where an exit route from a stair also forms the escape route from the ground and/or basement storeys, the width may need to be increased accordingly.

Calculation of minimum stair width

General

4.9 Every escape stair should be wide enough to accommodate the number of persons needing to use it in an emergency. This width will depend on the number of stairs provided and whether the escape strategy is based on the total evacuation of the building, or part of the building (see paragraph 4.15) or phased evacuation (see paragraph 4.19).

4.10 As with the design of horizontal escape routes, where the maximum number of people needing to use the escape stairs is not known, the appropriate capacity should be calculated on the basis of the occupant capacity. Guidance is set out in paragraph 0.38 and Table 1.

Discounting of stairs

4.11 Whether phased or total evacuation is used, where two or more stairs are provided it should be assumed that one of them might not be available due to fire or smoke. It is therefore necessary to discount each stair in turn in order to ensure that the capacity of the remaining stair(s) is adequate for the number of persons needing to escape.

4.12 An exception to the above discounting rule is if the escape stairs are approached on each storey through a protected lobby. In such a case the likelihood of a stair not being available is significantly reduced and it is not necessary to discount a stair. A protected lobby need not be provided on the topmost storey for the exception still to apply.

4.13 Another exception is if the stairways are protected by a smoke control system designed in accordance with BS 5588: Part 4.

4.14 The stair discounting rule applies to a building fitted with a sprinkler system, unless the stairs are lobbied or protected by a smoke control system, as in 4.12 or 4.13.

Total evacuation

4.15 In a building designed for total evacuation, the escape stairs (in conjunction with the rest of the means of escape) should have the capacity to allow all floors to be evacuated simultaneously. In calculating the width of the stairs account is taken of the number of people temporarily housed in the stairways during the evacuation.

4.16 Escape based on total evacuation should be used for:

a. all stairs serving basements;

b. all stairs serving buildings with open spatial planning; and

c. all stairs serving Other Residential or Assembly and recreation buildings.

4.17 Where total evacuation is to be used the capacity of stairs of widths from 1.0 to 1.8m, serving up to 10 storeys, is given in Table 7.

4.18 The widths for taller buildings than those covered by Table 7 can be derived from the formula: $P = 200w + 50 (w - 0.3)(n - 1)$ where: (P) is the number of people that can be accommodated; (w) is the width of the stair, in metres; and (n) is the number of storeys in the building.

Note that stairs with a rise of more than 30m should not be wider than 1.4m unless provided with a central handrail (see paragraph 4.6).

Worked example:
What is the total stair width needed (after discounting any one stairway) in a twelve storey building with a population of 1200 people (excluding the ground floor population which is assumed to use other exits), using total simultaneous evacuation?

$$i.e. \ P = 1200$$
$$n = 12$$

from the formula:

$$1200 = 200w + 50 (w - 0.3) (12 - 1)$$
$$1200 = 200w + 550w - 165$$
$$1365 = 750w$$
$$w = 1.82m$$

Therefore the total width of stairs, after discounting the largest one, should be at least 1.82m. Three 1.1m stairs would be necessary to meet the needs of discounting and the table 6 minimum width.

Table 7 Capacity of a stair for basements and for total evacuation of the building

No. of floors served	Maximum number of persons served by a stair of width:								
	1000mm	1100mm	1200mm	1300mm	1400mm	1500mm	1600mm	1700mm	1800mm
1.	150	220	240	260	280	300	320	340	360
2.	190	260	285	310	335	360	385	410	435
3.	230	300	330	360	390	420	450	480	510
4.	270	340	375	410	445	480	515	550	585
5.	310	380	420	460	500	540	580	620	660
6.	350	420	465	510	555	600	645	690	735
7.	390	460	510	560	610	660	710	760	810
8.	430	500	555	610	665	720	775	830	885
9.	470	540	600	660	720	780	840	900	960
10.	510	580	645	710	775	840	905	970	1035

Note:

The capacity of stairs serving more than 10 storeys may be obtained by using the formula in paragraph 4.18.

Phased evacuation

4.19 Where it is appropriate to do so, it may be advantageous to design stairs in high buildings on the basis of phased evacuation. In phased evacuation the first people to be evacuated are all those of reduced mobility and those on the storeys most immediately affected by the fire, usually the floor of fire origin and the floor above. Subsequently, if there is a need to evacuate more people, it is done two floors at a time. It is a method which cannot be used in every type of building, and it depends on the provision (and maintenance) of certain supporting facilities such as fire alarms. It does enable narrower stairs to be incorporated than would be the case if total evacuation were used, and has the practical advantage of reducing disruption in large buildings.

4.20 Phased evacuation should be used for buildings over 30m high unless they are identified in paragraph 4.16.

4.21 Buildings not identified in paragraph 4.16 which are less than 30m high may also be designed on the basis of phased evacuation if the conditions in paragraph 4.22 are met.

4.22 The following conditions should be met in a building or part of a building that is designed on the basis of phased evacuation:

a. the stairways should be approached through a protected lobby or protected corridor at each storey, except a top storey consisting exclusively of plant rooms;

b. every floor should be a compartment floor;

c. if the building has a storey with a floor over 30m above ground level, the building should be protected throughout by an automatic sprinkler system meeting the relevant recommendations of BS 5306 *Fire extinguishing installations and equipment on premises: Part 2: Specification for sprinkler systems*, ie. the relevant occupancy rating together with the additional requirements for life safety; this provision would not apply to any Purpose Group 1(a) (flats) part of a mixed use building;

d. the building should be fitted with an appropriate fire warning system, conforming to at least the L3 standard given in BS 5839: Part 1;

e. an internal speech communication system, such as a telephone or intercom system, should be provided to permit conversation between a control point at fire service access level, and a fire warden on every storey.

4.23 The minimum width of stair needed when phased evacuation is used is given in Table 8.

This table assumes a phased evacuation of not more than two floors at a time.

Table 8 Minimum aggregate width of stairs designed for phased evacuation

Maximum number of people in any storey	Stair width(1)mm
100	1000
120	1100
130	1200
140	1300
150	1400
160	1500
170	1600
180	1700
190	1800

Notes:

1. Stairs with a rise of more than 30m should not be wider than 1400mm unless provided with a central handrail (see para 4.6)

2. As an alternative to using this table, provided that the minimum width of a stair is at least 1000mm, the width may be calculated from: $[(P \times 10) - 100]$mm where P = the number of people on the most heavily occupied storey.

Protection of escape stairs

General
4.24 Escape stairs need to have a satisfactory standard of fire protection if they are to fulfil their role as areas of relative safety during a fire evacuation. The guidance in paragraph 4.25 to paragraph 4.33 should be followed to achieve this.

Enclosure of escape stairs
4.25 Every internal escape stair should be a protected stair (ie it should be within a fire resisting enclosure).

However an unprotected stair (an accommodation stair) may form part of an internal route to a storey exit or final exit, provided that the distance of travel and the number of people involved are very limited. Note, for example, the provisions for small shops in clause 9 of BS 5588: Part 2.

There may be additional measures if the protected stairway is also a protected shaft (where it penetrates one or more compartment floors, see Section 8) or if it is a firefighting shaft (see Section 17).

Access lobbies and corridors
4.26 There are situations where an escape stair needs the added protection of a protected lobby or protected corridor. These are :-

a. where the stair is the only one serving a building (or part of a building) which has more than one storey above or below the ground storey; or

b. where the stair serves any storey at a height greater than 20m ; or

c. where the building is designed for phased evacuation; or

d. in a sprinklered building in which the stair width has not been based on discounting one stairway (see paragraph 4.11).

In these cases protected lobbies or protected corridors are needed at all levels, except the top storey; and at all basement levels.

4.27 A protected lobby should be provided between an escape stairway and a place of special fire risk. In this case, the lobby should have not less than 0.4 m² permanent ventilation, or be protected from the ingress of smoke by a mechanical smoke control system.

Exits from protected stairways
4.28 Every protected stairway should discharge:

a. directly to a final exit; or

b. by way of a protected exit passageway to a final exit .

4.29 The exit from a protected stairway should be at least as wide as the stair leading to it.

Separation of adjoining stairways
4.30 Where two protected stairways are adjacent, they, and any protected exit passageways linking them to final exits, should be separated by an imperforate enclosure.

Use of space within protected stairways
4.31 A protected stairway needs to be free of potential sources of fire. Consequently, facilities that may be incorporated in a protected stairway are limited to the following:-

a. sanitary accommodation or washrooms, so long as the accommodation is not used as a cloakroom. A gas water heater or sanitary towel incinerator may be installed in the accommodation but not any other gas appliance;

b. a lift well may be included in a protected stairway, if it is not a firefighting stair;

c. a reception desk or enquiry office area at ground or access level, if it is not in the only stair serving the building or part of the building. The reception or enquiry office area should not be more than 10m² in area.

d. cupboards enclosed with fire resisting construction, if it is not in the only stair serving the building or part of the building.

External walls of protected stairways
4.32 The provisions in paragraph 2.38, and Diagram 13, apply equally to buildings other than dwellings.

Gas service pipes in protected stairways
4.33 The reference to gas service pipes or associated meters set out in paragraph 2.39, also applies to buildings other than dwellings.

Basement stairs

4.34 The guidance on basement stairs in paragraphs 2.40 to 2.42, also applies to buildings other than dwellings

External escape stairs

4.35 If more than one escape route is available from a storey, or part of a building, one of those routes may be by way of an external escape stair, provided that:

a. in the case of an Assembly and Recreation building, the route is not intended for use by members of the public; or

b. in the case of an Institutional building, the route serves only office or residential staff accommodation.

4.36 Where external stairs are acceptable as forming part of an escape route, it is important that the external stair is sufficiently protected from the weather and is adequately protected from a fire in the building. The guidance in paragraph 2.45 should be followed with the proviso that the stair may be more than 6m in vertical extent if it is protected from the effects of snow and ice.

Where weather protection is necessary, this should not be taken to imply a full enclosure.

Much will depend on the location of the stair and the degree of protection given to the stair by the building itself.

Section 5

GENERAL PROVISIONS COMMON TO BUILDINGS OTHER THAN DWELLINGHOUSES

Application of provisions in Section 5
5.1 This section gives guidance on the construction and protection of escape routes generally, and on some services installations and other matters associated with the design of escape routes. It applies to all buildings other than dwelling houses (refer to Section 1 for those).

It should therefore be read in conjunction with Section 2 (in respect of flats and maisonettes), and in conjunction with Sections 3 and 4 (in respect of other buildings).

Protection of escape routes

Fire resistance of enclosures
5.2 Details of fire resistance test criteria, and standards of performance, are set out in Appendix A. Generally a 30 minute standard is sufficient for the protection of means of escape. The exceptions to this are when greater fire resistance is required by the guidance on Requirements B3 or B5 or some other specific instance to meet Requirement B1, in Sections 3 and 4.

5.3 All walls, partitions and other enclosures that need to be fire-resisting to meet the provisions in this Approved Document (including roofs that form part of a means of escape), should have the appropriate performance given in Tables A1 and A2 of Appendix A.

5.4 Elements protecting a means of escape should meet any limitations on the use of glass (see paragraph 5.7).

Fire resistance of doors
5.5 Details of fire resistance test criteria, and standards of performance, are set out in Appendix B.

5.6 All doors that need to be fire-resisting to meet the provisions in this Approved Document should have the appropriate performance given in Table B1 of Appendix B.

Doors should also meet any limitations on the use of glass (see paragraph 5.7).

Fire resistance of glazed elements
5.7 Where glazed elements in fire-resisting enclosures and doors are only able to satisfy the relevant performance in terms of integrity, the use of glass is limited. These limitations are set out in Appendix A, Table A4.

5.8 Where the relevant performance can be met in terms of both integrity and insulation, there is no restriction in this Approved Document on the use or amount of glass, but there are some restrictions on the use of glass in firefighting stairs and lobbies under the recommendations in clause 9 in BS 5588: Part 5 for robust construction (which is referred to in Section 17).

5.9 Attention is also drawn to the guidance on the safety of glazing in the Approved Document to Part N, Glazing - materials and protection.

Doors on escape routes

5.10 The time taken to negotiate a closed door can be critical in escaping. Doors on escape routes (both within and from the building) should therefore be readily openable, if undue delay is to be avoided. Accordingly the following provisions in paragraphs 5.11 to 5.18 should be met.

Door fastenings
5.11 In general, doors on escape routes, whether or not the doors are fire doors, should either not be fitted with lock, latch or bolt fastenings, or they should only be fitted with simple fastenings that can be readily operated from the side approached by people making an escape. The operation of these fastenings should be without the use of a key and without having to manipulate more than one mechanism.

5.12 In buildings where security on final exit doors is an important consideration, such as in some Assembly and Recreation or Shop and Commercial uses, panic bolts may be used.

5.13 Guidance about door closing and 'hold open' devices for fire doors is given in Appendix B.

Direction of opening
5.14 The door of any doorway or exit should, if reasonably practicable, be hung to open in the direction of escape, and should always do so if the number of persons that might be expected to use the door at the time of a fire is more than 50.

Amount of opening and effect on associated escape routes
5.15 All doors on escape routes should be hung to open not less than 90 degrees, and with a swing that is clear of any change of floor level, other than a threshold or single step on the line of the doorway (see paragraph 5.21) and does not reduce the effective width of any escape route across a landing.

5.16 A door that opens towards a corridor or a stairway should be sufficiently recessed to prevent its swing from encroaching on the effective width of the stairway or corridor.

Vision panels in doors

5.17 Vision panels are needed where doors on escape routes sub-divide corridors, or where any doors are hung to swing both ways, but note also the provision in the Approved Document to Part M, Access and facilities for disabled people, concerning vision panels in doors across accessible corridors and passageways.

Revolving and automatic doors

5.18 Revolving doors, automatic doors and turnstiles can obstruct the passage of persons escaping. Accordingly, they should not be placed across escape routes unless they are arranged to fail safely in the open position or be easily openable in an emergency.

Alternatively, swing doors of the required width should be provided immediately adjacent to the revolving or automatic door.

Stairs

Construction of escape stairs

5.19 Every escape stair and its associated landings should be constructed of materials of limited combustibility in the following situations:

a. if it is the only stair serving the building, or part of the building, unless the building is of two or three storeys and is in Purpose Group 1(a).

b. if it is within a basement storey (this does not apply to a private stair in a maisonette).

c. if it serves any storey having a floor level more than 20m above ground or access level, or

d. if it is external, except in the case of a stair that connects the ground floor or paving level with a floor or flat roof not more than 6m above or below ground level.

There is further guidance on external escape stairs in paragraphs 2.45 and 4.35.

e. if it is a firefighting stair (see Section 17).

In satisfying the above conditions combustible materials may be added to the upper surface of these stairs (except in the case of firefighting stairs).

5.20 There is further guidance on the construction of firefighting stairs in Section 17. Dimensional constraints on the design of stairs generally, to meet requirements for safety in use, are given in Approved Document K, Stairs, ramps and guards.

Single steps

5.21 Single steps may cause falls and should only be used on escape routes where they are prominently marked. A single step on the line of a doorway is acceptable.

Helical stairs, spiral stairs and fixed ladders

5.22 Helical stairs, spiral stairs and fixed ladders may form part of an escape route subject to the following restrictions.

a. helical and spiral stairs should be designed in accordance with BS 5395 *Stairs, ladders and walkways:* Part 2 and, if they are intended to serve members of the public, should be a type E (public) stair, in accordance with that standard.

b. fixed ladders should not be used as a means of escape for members of the public, and should only be intended for use in circumstances where it is not practical to provide a conventional stair, for example as access to plant rooms that are not normally occupied. Fixed ladders should be constructed of non-combustible materials.

5.23 Guidance on the design of helical and spiral stairs, and fixed ladders, from the aspect of safety in use, is given in Approved Document K, Stairs, ramps and guards.

General

Height of escape routes

5.24 All escape routes should have a clear headroom of not less than 2 m and there should be no projection below this height (except for door frames).

Floors of escape routes

5.25 The floorings of all escape routes (including the treads of steps, and surfaces of ramps and landings) should be chosen to minimise their slipperiness when wet.

Ramps and sloping floors

5.26 Where a ramp forms part of an escape route it should have an easy gradient and in no case be steeper than 1 in 12.

5.27 Any sloping floor or tier should be constructed with a pitch of not more than 35° to the horizontal.

5.28 Further guidance on the design of ramps and associated landings, and on aisles and gangways in places where there is fixed seating, from the aspect of safety in use, is given in Approved Document K, Stairs, ramps and guards, and in Approved Document M, Access and facilities for disabled people. The design of means of escape in places with fixed seating is dealt with in Section 3 by reference to BS 5588: Part 6.

Final exits

5.29 Final exits need to be dimensioned and sited to facilitate the evacuation of persons out of and away from the building. Accordingly, they should be not less in width than the escape route(s) they serve and should also meet the conditions in the following paragraphs 5.30-5.32.

5.30 Final exits should be sited to ensure rapid dispersal of persons from the vicinity of the building so that they are no longer in danger from fire and smoke. Direct access to a street, passageway, walkway or open space should be available. The route clear of the building should be well defined, and if necessary suitably guarded.

5.31 Final exits need to be apparent to persons who may need to use them. This is particularly important where the exit opens off a stair that continues down, or up, beyond the level of the final exit.

5.32 Final exits should be sited so that they are clear of any risk from fire or smoke in a basement (such as the outlets to basement smoke vents- see Section 18), or from openings to transformer chambers, refuse chambers, boiler rooms and similar risks.

Lighting of escape routes

5.33 All escape routes should have adequate artificial lighting. Routes and areas listed in Table 9 should also have escape lighting which illuminates the route if the mains supply fails.

Lighting to escape stairs should be on a separate circuit from that supplying any other part of the escape route.

Standards for the installation of a system of escape lighting are given in BS 5266 *Emergency lighting: Part 1: 1988 Code of practice for the emergency lighting of premises other than cinemas and certain other specified premises used for entertainment,* and CP 1007: 1955 *Maintained lighting for cinemas.*

Exit signs

5.34 Except in dwellings, every doorway or other exit providing access to a means of escape, other than exits in ordinary use, should be distinctively and conspicuously marked by an exit sign, in letters of adequate size. Exit signs should be in accordance with BS 5499: Part 1: 1984. In some buildings additional signs may be needed to meet requirements under other legislation.

Protected power circuits

5.35 These are specified in a number of situations in this Approved Document where it is critical that electrical circuits are able to continue to function during a fire. A protected circuit for operation of equipment in the event of fire should consist of cable meeting the requirements for classification as CWZ in accordance with BS 6387. It should follow a route selected to pass only through parts of the building in which the fire risk is negligible and should be separate from any circuit provided for another purpose.

Table 9 Provisions for escape lighting

Purpose group of the building or part of the building	Areas requiring escape lighting
Residential	All common escape routes
Office, Shop and Commercial(1), Industrial, Storage, Other non-residential	a. Underground or windowless accommodation b. Stairways in a central core or serving storey(s) more than 20m above ground level c. Internal corridors more than 30m long d. Open-plan office areas of more than 60m²
Shop and Commercial(2) and car parks to which the public are admitted	All escape routes (except in shops of 3 or fewer storeys with no sales floor more than 280m² provided that the shop is not a restaurant or bar)
Assembly and Recreation	All escape routes and accommodation except for: a. accommodation open on one side to view sport or entertainment during normal daylight hours b. toilet accommodation having a gross floor area not more than 8m²
Any purpose group	a. electricity generator rooms b. switch room/battery room for emergency lighting system c. emergency control room

Notes:

1. Those parts of the premises to which the public are not admitted
2. Those parts of the premises to which the public are admitted

---

Lifts

Evacuation lifts

5.36 In general it is not appropriate to use lifts when there is a fire in the building because there is always the danger of people being trapped in a lift that has become immobilised as a result of the fire. However, in some circumstances a lift may be provided as part of a management plan for evacuating disabled persons. In such cases the lift installation needs to be appropriately sited and protected, and needs to contain a number of safety features that are intended to ensure that the lift remains usable for evacuation purposes during the fire.

Guidance on the necessary measures is given in BS 5588: Part 8.

Fire protection of lift installations

5.37 Because lifts connect floors, there is the possibility that they may prejudice escape routes. To safeguard against this, the following conditions in paragraphs 5.38 to 5.42 should be met.

5.38 Lifts, such as wall-climber or feature lifts which rise within a large volume such as a mall or atrium, and do not have a conventional well, may be at risk if they run through a smoke reservoir. In which case care is needed to maintain the integrity of the smoke reservoir, and protect the occupants of the lift.

5.39 Lift wells should be either contained within the enclosures of a protected stairway, or be enclosed throughout their height with fire-resisting construction if they are sited so as to prejudice the means of escape. A lift well connecting different compartments should form a protected shaft (see Section 8).

5.40 In basements and enclosed car parks the lift should be approached only by a protected lobby (or protected corridor) unless it is within the enclosure of a protected stairway.

This is also the case in any storey that contains high fire risk areas, if the lift also delivers directly into corridors serving sleeping accommodation. Examples of fire risk areas in this context are kitchens, lounges and stores.

5.41 A lift should not be continued down to serve any basement storey if it is in a building (or part of a building) served by only one escape stair, or if it is within the enclosures to an escape stair which is terminated at ground level.

5.42 Lift machine rooms should be sited over the lift well whenever possible. If the lift well is within a protected stairway which is the only stairway serving the building (or part of the building), then if the machine room cannot be sited above the lift well it should be located outside the stairway (to avoid smoke spread from a fire in the machine room).

Mechanical ventilation and air conditioning systems

5.43 Any system of mechanical ventilation should be designed to ensure that in a fire the air movement in the building is directed away from protected escape routes and exits, or that the system (or an appropriate section of it) is closed down. In the case of a system which recirculates air, it should meet the relevant recommendation for recirculating distribution systems in BS 5588: Part 9: 1989, in terms of its operation under fire conditions.

5.44 Guidance on the use of mechanical ventilation in a place of assembly is given in BS 5588: Part 6.

5.45 Where a pressurization system is installed, ventilation and air conditioning systems in the building should be compatible with it when operating under fire conditions.

5.46 Guidance on the design and installation of mechanical ventilation and air conditioning plant is given in BS 5720, and on ventilation and air conditioning ductwork in BS 5588: Part 9.

Refuse chutes and storage

5.47 Refuse storage chambers, refuse chutes and refuse hoppers should be sited and constructed in accordance with BS 5906.

5.48 Refuse chutes and rooms provided for the storage of refuse should:

a.   be separated from other parts of the building by fire-resisting construction, and

b.   not be located within protected stairways or protected lobbies;

5.49 Rooms containing refuse chutes, or provided for the storage of refuse, should be approached either directly from the open air or by way of a protected lobby provided with not less than 0.2m² of permanent ventilation.

5.50 Access to refuse storage chambers should not be sited adjacent to escape routes or final exits, or near to windows of dwellings.

The Requirement

This Approved Document which takes effect on
1 June 1992, deals with the following
Requirement from Part B of Schedule 1 to the
Building Regulations 1991.

Requirement	*Limits on application*
Internal fire spread (linings) **B2** (1) To inhibit the spread of fire within the building the internal linings shall- (a) resist the spread of flame over their surfaces; and (b) have, if ignited, a rate of heat release which is reasonable in the circumstances (2) In this paragraph "internal linings" mean the materials lining any partition, wall, ceiling or other internal structure.	

Performance

In the Secretary of State's view the requirement of B2 will be met if the spread of flame over the internal linings of the building is restricted by making provision for them to have low rates of surface spread of flame, and in some cases to have a low rate of heat release, so as to limit the contribution that the fabric of the building makes to fire growth. The extent to which this is necessary is dependent on the location of the lining.

Introduction

Fire spread and lining materials

*0.41 The choice of materials for walls and ceilings can significantly affect the spread of a fire and its rate of growth, even though they are not likely to be the materials first ignited.

It is particularly important in circulation spaces where linings may offer the main means by which fire spreads, and where rapid spread is most likely to prevent occupants from escaping.

Two properties of lining materials that influence fire spread are the rate of flame spread over the surface when it is subject to intense radiant heating, and the rate at which the lining material gives off heat when burning. The guidance in this document provides for control of internal fire spread through control of these properties. This document does not give guidance on other properties such as the generation of smoke and fumes.

Floors and stairs

0.42 The provisions do not apply to the upper surfaces of floors and stairs because they are not significantly involved in a fire until it is well developed, and thus do not play an important part in fire spread in the early stages of a fire that are most relevant to the safety of occupants.

Other controls on internal surface properties

0.43 There is also guidance on the control of flame spread inside buildings in two other Sections. In Section 9 there is guidance on surfaces exposed in concealed spaces above fire-protecting suspended ceilings, and in Section 10 on enclosures to above ground drainage system pipes. In Section 14 there is

guidance on the internal surfaces of rooflights in connection with the performance of roof coverings. External flame spread is dealt with in Sections 12-14.

Furniture and fittings

0.44 Furniture and fittings can have a major effect on fire spread but it is not possible to control them through Building Regulations, and they are not dealt with in this Approved Document. Fire characteristics of furniture and fittings may be controlled in some buildings under legislation that applies to a building in use, such as licensing arrangements.

Classification of performance

0.45 Appendix A describes the different classes of performance and the appropriate methods of test. The main classifications used are based on tests in BS 476: *Fire tests on building materials and structures* Part 6: *Method of test for fire propagation for products* and Part 7: *Method for classification of surface spread of flame of products.* Other tests are available for classification of thermoplastic materials if they do not have the appropriate rating under BS 476 Part 7 and three ratings, referred to as TP(a) and TP(a) flexible and TP(b), are used.

Table A8, in Appendix A, gives typical performance ratings which may be achieved by some generic materials and products.

* Introductory paragraphs 0.18 - 0.40 are on pages 10-13

Section 6

WALL AND CEILING LININGS

Classification of linings

6.1 Subject to the variations and specific provisions described in paragraphs 6.2 to 6.9 below, the surface linings of walls and ceilings should meet the following classifications:-

Table 10 **Classification of linings**	
Location	**Class**
Small rooms of area not more than 4m² in a residential building and 30m² in a non-residential building	3
Other rooms	1
Circulation spaces within dwellings	
Other circulation spaces, including the common areas of flats and maisonettes	0

Definition of walls

6.2 For the purpose of the performance of wall linings, a wall includes:

a. the surface of glazing (except glazing in doors), and

b. any part of a ceiling which slopes at an angle of more than 70° to the horizontal.

But a wall does not include:

c. doors and door frames,

d. window frames and frames in which glazing is fitted,

e. architraves, cover moulds, picture rails, skirtings and similar narrow members, and

f. fireplace surrounds, mantleshelves and fitted furniture.

Definition of ceilings

6.3 For the purposes of the performance of ceiling linings a ceiling includes:

a. the surface of glazing

b. any part of a wall which slopes at an angle of 70° or less to the horizontal.

But a ceiling does not include:

c. trap doors and their frames,

d. the frames of windows or rooflights (see Appendix E) and frames in which glazing is fitted,

e. architraves, cover moulds, picture rails, and similar narrow members

Variations and special provisions

Walls
6.4 Parts of walls in rooms may be of a lower class than specified in paragraph 6.1 (but not lower than Class 3) provided the total area of those parts in any one room does not exceed one half of the floor area of the room, subject to a maximum of 20m² in a residential building, and 60m² in a non-residential building.

Fire-protecting suspended ceilings
6.5 A suspended ceiling can contribute to the overall fire resistance of a floor/ceiling assembly. Such a ceiling should satisfy paragraph 6.1. If the assembly is to achieve 60 minutes fire resistance or more, it should also meet the provisions of Appendix A table A3, for a type D ceiling.

Fire-resisting ceilings
6.6 Cavity barriers are needed in some concealed floor or roof spaces (see Section 9), however this need can be reduced by the use of a fire-resisting ceiling below the cavity. Such a ceiling should comply with Diagram 31 which stipulates a Class 0 surface on the soffit.

Rooflights
6.7 Rooflights should meet the relevant classification in 6.1. However plastic rooflights with at least a class 3 rating may be used where 6.1 calls for a higher standard, provided the limitations in table 11 below and in table 18 are observed.

Thermoplastic materials

General
6.8 Thermoplastic materials (see Appendix A paragraph A16) which cannot meet the performance given in Table 10, can nevertheless be used in rooflights and lighting diffusers in suspended ceilings if they comply with the provisions described in paragraphs 6.9 to 6.11 below. Flexible thermoplastic material may be used in panels to form a suspended ceiling if it complies with the guidance in paragraph 6.14. The classifications used in paragraph 6.9 - 6.12, Table 11 and Diagram 21 are explained in Appendix A paragraph A19.

Windows
6.9 External windows to rooms (though not to circulation spaces) may be glazed with thermoplastic materials, if the material can be classified as a TP(a) rigid product.

Internal glazing should meet the provisions in paragraph 6.1 above. (Note that a wall does not include glazing in a door, see paragraph 6.2).

Rooflights

6.10 Rooflights to rooms and circulation spaces (with the exception of protected stairways) may be constructed of a thermoplastic material if:

a. the lower surface has a TP(a) (rigid) or TP(b) classification,

b. the size and disposition of the rooflights accords with the limitations in Table 11 and with the guidance to B4 in table 18.

Lighting diffusers

6.11 The following provisions apply only to lighting diffusers which form part of a ceiling, and are not concerned with diffusers of light fittings which are attached to the soffit of, or suspended beneath a ceiling (see Diagram 20).

Lighting diffusers are translucent or open-structured elements that allow light to pass through. They may be part of a luminaire or used below rooflights or other sources of light.

6.12 Thermoplastic lighting diffusers should not be used in fire protecting or fire resisting ceilings, unless they have been satisfactorily tested as part of the ceiling system that is to be used to provide the appropriate fire protection.

6.13 Subject to the above paragraphs, ceilings to rooms and circulation spaces (but not protected stairways) may incorporate thermoplastic lighting diffusers if the following provisions are observed:-

a. Wall and ceiling surfaces exposed within the space above the suspended ceiling (other than the upper surfaces of the thermoplastic panels) should comply with the general provisions of paragraph 6.1, according to the type of space below the suspended ceiling.

b. If the diffusers are of classification TP (a) (rigid), there are no restrictions on their extent

c. If the diffusers are of classification TP(b), they should be limited in extent as indicated in Table 11 and Diagram 21.

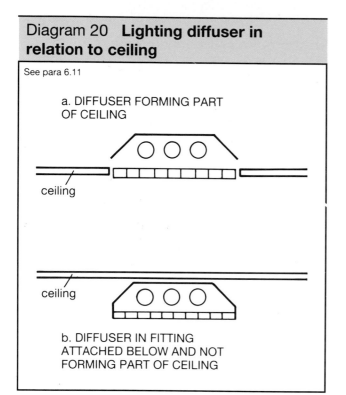

Diagram 20 Lighting diffuser in relation to ceiling

See para 6.11

a. DIFFUSER FORMING PART OF CEILING

ceiling

ceiling

b. DIFFUSER IN FITTING ATTACHED BELOW AND NOT FORMING PART OF CEILING

Table 11 Limitations applied to thermoplastic rooflights and lighting diffusers in suspended ceiling and Class 3 plastics rooflights

Minimum classification of lower surface	Use of space below the diffusers or rooflight	Maximum area of each diffuser panel or rooflight(1)	Max total area of diffuser panels and rooflights as percentage of floor area of the space in which the ceiling is located	Minimum separation distance between diffuser panels or rooflights(1)
TP(a)	any except protected stairway	No limit(2)	No limit	No limit
Class 3(3) or TP(b)	rooms	5 sq.m	50	3m
	circulation spaces except protected stairways	5 sq.m	15	3m

Note:

1. Smaller panels can be grouped together provided that the overall size of the group and the space between one group and any others satisfies the dimensions shown in Diagram 21.

2. Lighting diffusers of TP(a) flexible rating should be restricted to panels of not more than 5 sq.m each, see paragraph 6.14.

3. There are no limitations on Class 3 material in small rooms.

Diagram 21 Layout restrictions on Class 3 plastic rooflights, TP(b) rooflights and TP(b) lighting diffusers

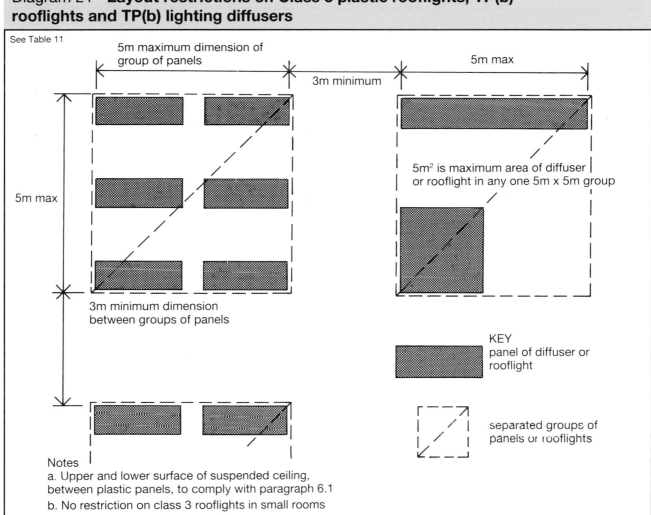

See Table 11

5m maximum dimension of group of panels

3m minimum

5m max

5m max

$5m^2$ is maximum area of diffuser or rooflight in any one 5m x 5m group

3m minimum dimension between groups of panels

KEY
panel of diffuser or rooflight

separated groups of panels or rooflights

Notes
a. Upper and lower surface of suspended ceiling, between plastic panels, to comply with paragraph 6.1
b. No restriction on class 3 rooflights in small rooms

Suspended or stretched-skin ceilings

6.14 The ceiling of a room may be constructed either as a suspended or stretched skin membrane from panels of a thermoplastic material of the TP (a) flexible classification, provided that it is not part of a fire resisting ceiling. Each panel should not exceed $5m^2$ in area and should be supported on all its sides.

The Requirement

This Approved Document which takes effect on
1 June 1992, deals with the following
Requirement from Part B of Schedule 1 to the
Building Regulations 1991.

Requirement	Limits on application
Internal fire spread (structure) **B3** (1) The building shall be designed and constructed so that, in the event of fire, its stability will be maintained for a reasonable period. (2) A wall common to two or more buildings shall be designed and constructed so that it resists the spread of fire between those buildings. For the purposes of this sub-paragraph a house in a terrace and a semi-detached house are each to be treated as a separate building. (3) To inhibit the spread of fire within the building, it shall be sub-divided with fire-resisting construction to an extent appropriate to the size and intended use of the building. (4) The building shall be designed and constructed so that the unseen spread of fire and smoke within concealed spaces in its structure and fabric is inhibited.	Requirement B3(3) does not apply to material alterations to any prison provided under section 33 of the Prisons Act 1952.

Guidance

Performance

In the Secretary of State's view the requirements of B3 will be met:

a. if the load bearing elements of structure of the building are capable of withstanding the effects of fire for an appropriate period without loss of stability,

b. if the building is sub-divided by elements of fire-resisting construction into compartments,

c. if any openings in fire separating elements are suitably protected in order to maintain the fire integrity of the element, and

d. if any hidden voids in the construction are sealed and subdivided to inhibit the unseen spread of fire and products of combustion, in order to reduce the risk of structural failure, and the spread of fire, in so far as they pose a threat to the safety of people in and around the building.

The extent to which any of these measures are necessary is dependent on the use of the building, and in some cases its size, and on the location of the element of construction.

Introduction

*0.46 Guidance on loadbearing elements of structure is given in Section 7. Section 8 is concerned with the subdivision of a building into compartments, and Section 9 makes provisions about concealed spaces (or cavities). Section 10 gives information on the protection of openings and on fire-stopping which relates to compartmentation and to fire spread in concealed spaces. Section 11 is concerned with special measures which apply to car parks and shopping complexes. Common to all these sections, and to other provisions of Part B, is the property of fire resistance.

Fire resistance

0.47 The fire resistance of an element of construction is a measure of its ability to withstand the effects of fire in one or more ways, as follows:

a. resistance to collapse, ie the ability to maintain loadbearing capacity (which applies to loadbearing elements only);

b. resistance to fire penetration, ie an ability to maintain the integrity of the element (which applies to fire-separating elements);

c. resistance to the transfer of excessive heat, ie an ability to provide insulation from high temperatures (which applies to fire separating elements).

"Elements of structure" is the term applied to the main structural loadbearing elements, such as structural frames, floors and loadbearing walls. Compartment walls are treated as elements of structure although they are not necessarily loadbearing. Roofs, unless they serve the function of a floor, are not treated as elements of structure. External walls such as curtain walls or other forms of cladding which transmit only self weight and wind loads and do not transmit floor load are not regarded as loadbearing for the purposes of 0.47a, although they may need fire resistance to satisfy requirement B4 (see sections 12 - 14).

Loadbearing elements may or may not have a fire separating function. Similarly, fire separating elements may or may not be loadbearing.

Guidance elsewhere in the Approved Document concerning fire resistance

0.48 There is guidance in Sections 1-5 concerning the use of fire-resisting construction to protect means of escape. There is guidance in Section 12 about fire resistance of external walls to restrict the spread of fire between buildings. There is guidance in Section 17 about fire resistance in the construction of fire fighting shafts. Appendix A gives information on methods of test and performance for elements of construction. Appendix B gives information on fire-resisting doors. Appendix C gives information on methods of measurement. Appendix D gives information on purpose group classification. Appendix E gives definitions.

* Introduction paragraphs 0.41-0.45 are on page 46.

Section 7

LOADBEARING ELEMENTS OF STRUCTURE

7.1 Premature failure of the structure can be prevented by provisions for loadbearing elements of structure to have a minimum standard of fire resistance, in terms of resistance to collapse or failure of loadbearing capacity. The purpose in providing the structure with fire resistance is threefold, namely:

a. to minimise the risk to the occupants, some of whom may have to remain in the building for some time while evacuation proceeds if the building is a large one;

b. to reduce the risk to fire fighters, who may be engaged on search or rescue operations;

c. to reduce the danger to people in the vicinity of the building, who might be hurt by falling debris or as a result of the impact of the collapsing structure on other buildings.

Fire resistance standard

7.2 Structural frames, beams, columns, loadbearing walls (internal and external), floor structures and gallery structures, should have at least the fire resistance given in Appendix A, Table A1.

Application of the fire resistance standards for loadbearing elements.

7.3 The measures set out in Appendix A include provisions to ensure that where one element of structure supports or gives stability to another element of structure, the supporting element has no less fire resistance than the other element. The measures also provide for elements of structure that are common to more than one building or compartment, to be constructed to the standard of the greater of the relevant provisions. Special provisions about fire resistance of elements of structure in single storey buildings are also given, and there are concessions in respect of fire resistance of elements of structure in basements where at least one side of the basement is open at ground level.

Exclusions from the provisions for elements of structure

7.4 The following are excluded from the definition of elements of structure for the purposes of these provisions :

a. structure that only supports a roof, unless:

i. the roof performs the function of a floor, such as for parking vehicles, or as a means of escape (see Sections 1-5), or

ii. the structure is essential for the stability of an external wall which needs to have fire resistance.

b. the lowest floor of the building; and

c. a platform floor.

Additional guidance

7.5 Guidance in other sections of this Approved Document may also apply if a loadbearing wall is:

a. a compartment wall (this includes a wall common to two buildings); (see Section 8);

b. a wall between a house and a domestic garage; (see Section 8, paragraph 8.12);

c . protecting a means of escape; (see Sections 1-5);

d. an external wall; (see Section 12 & 13); or

e. enclosing a firefighting shaft; (see Section 17).

7.6 If a floor is also a compartment floor, see Section 8.

Floors in domestic loft conversions

7.7 In altering an existing two storey single family dwellinghouse to provide additional storeys, the provisions in this Approved Document are for the floor(s), both old and new, to have the full 30 minute standard of fire resistance shown in Appendix A, Table A1. However provided that the following conditions are satisfied, namely:

a. only one storey is being added;

b. the new storey contains no more than 2 habitable rooms; and,

c. the total area of the new storey does not amount to more than 50m^2;

then the existing first floor construction may be accepted if it has at least a modified 30 minute standard of fire resistance, in those places where:

d. the floor separates only rooms (and not circulation spaces); provided that

e. the provisions in Section 1, are met.

The 'modified 30 minute' standard satisfies the test criteria for the full 30 minutes in respect of loadbearing capacity, but allows reduced performances for integrity and insulation (see Appendix A Table A1, item 3(a)).

Raised storage areas

7.8 Raised free standing floors (which may be supported by racking) are frequently erected in single storey industrial buildings. Whether the structure is considered as a gallery or is of sufficient size that it is considered as a floor forming an additional storey, the provisions for fire resistance of elements of structure set out in Appendix A, Table A1, would apply to the structure.

7.9 In the case of automated storage systems in which people do not normally go onto any of the raised storage tiers, it may not be necessary to provide the storage structure with fire resistance to ensure the safety of occupants of the building.

7.10 Where people do go onto the storage tiers in the course of their normal use, reduced levels of fire resistance in the construction of the raised storage platforms (or even little fire resistance, so as to permit an unprotected steel structure) may also be acceptable provided the following conditions are satisfied:

a. the structure has only one tier and is used for storage purposes only;

b. the number of persons likely to be on the floor at any one time Is low and does not include members of the public;

c. the design is such that any persons on the floor would be readily aware of any fire starting at the lower level (see paragraph 7.11); and

d. at least one stair serving the floor should discharge within 4.5m of an exit from the building.

7.11 Features of layout or design that would allow occupants to be aware of a fire starting at the lower level include the use of perforations in the floor of the structure, or leaving a space between the edge of the platform and the walls of the room housing it, to make the smoke and the sounds of fire obvious. If the floor is more than 10m in width or length, an automatic detection and alarm system should be used to provide early warning.

Conversion to flats

7.12 Where an existing house or other building is converted into flats there is a material change of use to which Part B of the regulations applies. Where the existing building has timber floors and these are to be retained, the relevant provisions for fire resistance may be difficult to meet.

7.13 Provided that the means of escape conform to section 2, and are adequatly protected, a 30 minute standard of fire resistance could be accepted for the elements of structure in a building having not more than 3 storeys.

Where the altered building has 4 or more storeys the full standard of fire resistance given in Appendix A would normally be necessary.

Section 8

COMPARTMENTATION

Introduction

8.1 The spread of fire within a building can be restricted by sub-dividing it into compartments separated from one another by walls and/or floors of fire-resisting construction. The object is twofold:

a. to prevent rapid fire spread which could trap occupants of the building; and

b. to reduce the chance of fires becoming large, on the basis that large fires are more dangerous, not only to occupants and fire service personnel, but to people in the vicinity of the building. Compartmentation is complementary to provisions made in Sections 1-5 for the protection of escape routes, and to provisions made in Section 12-14 against the spread of fire between buildings.

8.2 The appropriate degree of sub-division depends on:

a. the use of, and fire load in, the building; which affects the potential for fires and the severity of fires, as well as the ease of evacuation;

b. the height to the floor of the top storey in the building, which is an indication of the ease of evacuation and the ability of the fire service to intervene effectively; and

c. the availability of a sprinkler system which affects the growth rate of the fire, and may suppress it altogether.

8.3 Sub-division is achieved using compartment walls and compartment floors, and provisions for their construction are given in paragraphs 8.19 et seq. These construction provisions vary according to the function of the wall or floor .

Special forms of compartmentation

8.4 Special forms of compartmentation to which particular construction provisions apply, are:

a. walls common to two or more buildings;

b. walls dividing buildings into separated parts in which the parts can be assessed independently for the purpose of determining the appropriate standard of fire resistance, see also paragraph 8.21; and

c. construction protecting houses from attached or integral domestic garages, see paragraph 8.12.

Junctions

8.5 For compartmentation to be effective, there should be continuity at the junctions of the fire-resisting elements enclosing a compartment, and any openings from one compartment to another should not present a weakness.

Protected shafts

8.6 Spaces that connect compartments, such as stairways and service shafts, need to be protected to restrict fire spread between the compartments, and they are termed protected shafts. Any walls or floors bounding a protected shaft are considered to be compartment walls or floors, for the purpose of this Approved Document.

Provision of compartmentation

General

8.7 Compartment walls and compartment floors should be provided in the circumstances described below, with the provison that the lowest floor in a building does not need to be constructed as a compartment floor. Paragraphs 8.8-8.18 give guidance on the provision of compartmentation in different building types. Information on the construction of compartment walls and compartment floors in different circumstances is given in paragraphs 8.19 et seq. Provisions for the protection of openings in compartment walls and compartment floors are given in paragraphs 8.28 et seq.

All purpose groups

8.8 A wall common to two or more buildings should be constructed as a compartment wall.

8.9 Parts of a building that are occupied mainly for different purposes, should be separated from one another by compartment walls and/or compartment floors. This does not apply where one of the different purposes is ancillary to the other. Refer to Appendix D for guidance on whether a function should be regarded as ancillary or not.

8.10 A wall or floor provided to divide a building into separate occupancies should also be constructed as a compartment wall or compartment floor.

Compartmentation in houses

8.11 Any wall separating semi-detached houses, or houses in terraces, should be constructed as a compartment wall, and the houses should be considered as separate buildings.

8.12 If a domestic garage is attached to (or forms an integral part of) a house, the garage should be separated from the rest of the house, as shown in Diagram 22.

Diagram 22 Separation between garage and dwellinghouse

See para 8.12

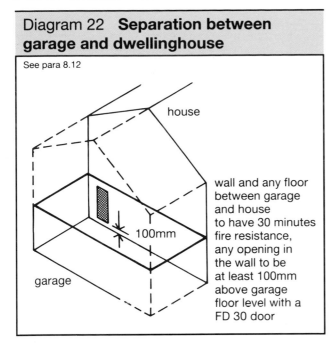

house

wall and any floor between garage and house to have 30 minutes fire resistance, any opening in the wall to be at least 100mm above garage floor level with a FD 30 door

100mm

garage

Compartmentation in flats

8.13 In buildings containing flats or maisonettes the following should be constructed as compartment walls or compartment floors:

a. any floor (unless it is within a maisonette, ie between one storey and another within one dwelling), and

b. any wall separating a flat or maisonette from any other part of the building, and

c. any wall enclosing a refuse storage chamber.

Compartmentation in institutional buildings including health care

8.14 In Institutional purpose group buildings, all floors should be constructed as compartment floors.

8.15 Compartments should not exceed $2000m^2$ in multi-storey hospitals and $3000m^2$ in single storey hospitals.

8.16 Any walls needed to divide the storeys of health care buildings into at least two compartments to comply with the means of escape provisions in Section 3.26 et seq, should be constructed as compartment walls.

Compartmentation in other residential buildings

8.17 All floors in buildings of the Other Residential purpose group should be constructed as compartment floors.

Diagram 23 Compartment walls and compartment floors with references to relevant paragraphs in Section 8

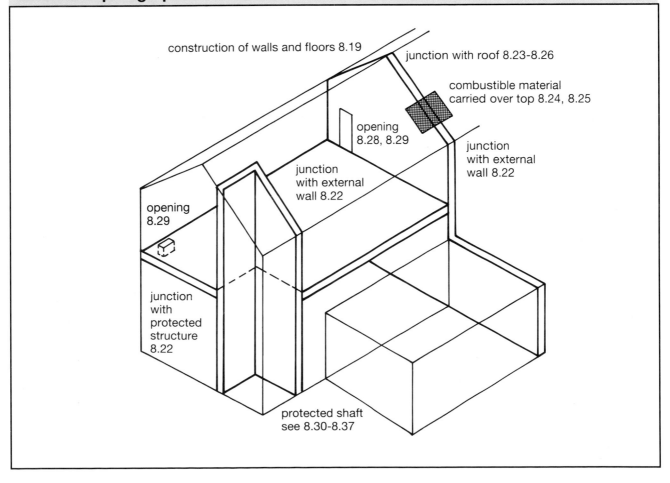

construction of walls and floors 8.19

junction with roof 8.23-8.26

combustible material carried over top 8.24, 8.25

opening 8.28, 8.29

junction with external wall 8.22

junction with external wall 8.22

opening 8.29

junction with protected structure 8.22

protected shaft see 8.30-8.37

Table 12 Maximum dimensions of building or compartment (multi-storey non-residential buildings)

Purpose group of building (or part)	Height of floor of top storey above ground level (m)	Floor area of any one storey in the building or compartment (m²)
Office	no limit	no limit
Assembly & Recreation Shop & Commercial:		
not sprinklered	no limit	2000
sprinklered (1)	no limit	4000
Industrial (3):		
not sprinklered	not more than 20	7000
	more than 20	2000 (2)
sprinklered (1)	not more than 20	14000
	more than 20	4000 (2)

	Height of floor of top storey above ground level (m)	Maximum compartment volume (m³)
Storage(3) & Other non-residential:		
a. car park for light vehicles	no limit	no limit
b. any other building or part:		
-not sprinklered	not more than 20	20000
	more than 20	4000 (2)
-sprinklered(1)	not more than 20	40000
	more than 20	8000 (2)

Notes:
1. "Sprinklered" means that the building is fitted throughout with an automatic sprinkler system meeting the relevant recommendations of BS5306: Part 2, ie the relevant occupancy rating together with the additional requirements for life safety.
2. This reduced area limit applies only to storeys that are more than 20m above ground level.
3. There may be additional limitations on floor area and/or sprinkler provisions in certain industrial and storage uses under other legislation, for example in respect of storage of LPG and certain chemicals.

Compartmentation in non-residential buildings

8.18 The following walls and floors should be constructed as compartment walls and compartment floors in buildings of a non-residential purpose group (ie Office, Shop & Commercial, Assembly & Recreation, Industrial, Storage or Other non - residential):

a.   any wall (unless the building is a single storey building) needed to sub-divide the building to observe the size limits on compartments given in Table 12;

b.   any floor if the building, or separated part (see paragraph 8.4) of the building, has a storey with a floor at a height of more than 30m above ground level;

c.   the floor of the ground storey if the building has one or more basements;

d.   any basement floor if the building, or separated part (see paragraph 8.4), has a basement at a depth of more than 10m below ground level; and

e.   if the building forms part of a Shopping Complex, any wall and floor described in Section 5 of BS 5588: part 10 as needing to be constructed to the standard for a compartment wall or compartment floor.

Construction of compartment walls and compartment floors

General

8.19 Every compartment wall and compartment floor should:

a.   form a complete barrier to fire between the compartments they separate; and

b.   have the appropriate fire resistance as indicated in Appendix A, Tables, A1 and A2.

Compartment walls between buildings

8.20 Compartment walls that are common to two or more buildings should run the full height of the building in a continuous vertical plane. Thus adjoining buildings should only be separated by walls, not floors. A compartment wall being used to divide a building into separate occupancies would not be subject to this provision.

Separated parts of buildings

8.21 Compartment walls used to form a separated part of a building should run the full height of the building in a continuous vertical plane. The concept of separated part is described in paragraph 8.4. The two separated parts can have different standards of fire resistance.

Junction of compartment wall or compartment floor with other walls

8.22 Where a compartment wall or compartment floor meets another compartment wall, or an external wall, the junction should maintain the fire resistance of the compartmentation.

Junction of compartment wall with roof

8.23 A compartment wall should be taken up to meet the underside of the roof covering or deck, with fire-stopping where necessary at the wall/roof junction to maintain the continuity of fire resistance.

8.24 If a fire penetrates a roof near a compartment wall there is a risk that it will spread over the roof to the adjoining compartment. To reduce this risk, and subject to 8.25 below, a zone of the roof 1.5m wide on either side of the wall should have a covering of designation AA, AB or AC (see Appendix A, paragraph A6) on a substrate or deck of a material of limited combustibility, as set out in Diagram 24a.

8.25 In buildings not more than 15m high, of the purpose groups listed below, combustible boarding used as a substrate to the roof covering, wood wool slabs, or timber tiling battens, may be carried over the compartment wall provided that they are fully bedded in mortar or other suitable material over the width of the wall (see Diagram 24b). This applies to: dwellinghouses, buildings or compartments in residential use (other than Institutional), Office buildings, Assembly and recreation buildings.

8.26 As an alternative to 8.24 or 8.25 the compartment wall may be extended up through the roof for a height of at least 375mm above the top surface of the adjoining roof covering.

Compartment construction in hospitals

8.27 Compartment walls and floors in hospitals designed on the basis of Firecode (see 0.34) should be constructed of material of limited combustibility if they have fire resistance of 60 minutes or more.

Openings in compartmentation

Openings in compartment walls separating buildings or occupancies

8.28 Any openings in a compartment wall which is common to two or more buildings, or between different occupancies in the same building, should be limited to those for:

Diagram 24 Junction of compartment wall with roof

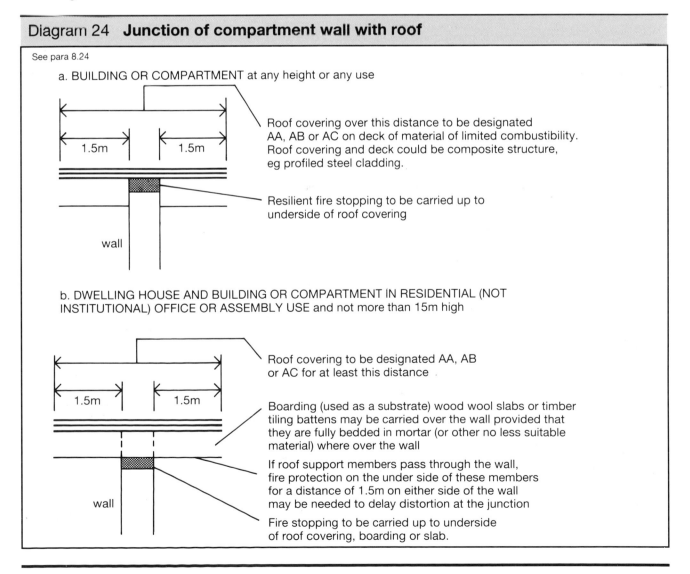

See para 8.24

a. BUILDING OR COMPARTMENT at any height or any use

1.5m   1.5m

Roof covering over this distance to be designated AA, AB or AC on deck of material of limited combustibility. Roof covering and deck could be composite structure, eg profiled steel cladding.

Resilient fire stopping to be carried up to underside of roof covering

wall

b. DWELLING HOUSE AND BUILDING OR COMPARTMENT IN RESIDENTIAL (NOT INSTITUTIONAL) OFFICE OR ASSEMBLY USE and not more than 15m high

1.5m   1.5m

Roof covering to be designated AA, AB or AC for at least this distance

Boarding (used as a substrate) wood wool slabs or timber tiling battens may be carried over the wall provided that they are fully bedded in mortar (or other no less suitable material) where over the wall

If roof support members pass through the wall, fire protection on the under side of these members for a distance of 1.5m on either side of the wall may be needed to delay distortion at the junction

Fire stopping to be carried up to underside of roof covering, boarding or slab.

wall

---

a.   a door which is needed to provide a means of escape in case of fire and which has the same fire resistance as that required for the wall (see Appendix B, Table B1) and is fitted in accordance with the provisions of Appendix B;

b.   the passage of a pipe which meets the provisions in Section 10.

Information on fire doors will be found in Appendix B

Openings in other compartment walls or in compartment floors

8.29 Openings in compartment walls (other than those described in paragraph 8.28) or compartment floors should be limited to those for:

a.   doors which have the appropriate fire resistance given in Appendix B, Table B1, and are fitted in accordance with the provisions of Appendix B; and

b.   the passage of pipes, ventilation ducts, chimneys, appliance ventilation ducts or ducts encasing one or more flue pipes, which meet the provisions in Section 10; and

c.   refuse chutes of non-combustible construction; and

d.   protected shafts which meet the relevant provisions below.

Protected shafts

8.30 Any stairway or other shaft passing directly from one compartment to another, should be enclosed in a protected shaft so as to delay or prevent the spread of fire between compartments.

There are additional provisions in Sections 1 - 5 for protected shafts that are protected stairways, and in Sections 15 - 18 if the stairway also serves as a firefighting stairway.

Uses for protected shafts

8.31 The uses of protected shafts should be restricted to stairs, lifts, escalators, chutes, ducts, and pipes. Sanitary accommodation and washrooms may be included in protected shafts.

Construction of protected shafts

8.32 The construction enclosing a protected shaft (see Diagram 25) should:

a.   form a complete barrier to fire between the different compartments which the shaft connects;

b.   have the appropriate fire resistance given in Appendix A, Table A1, except for glazed screens which meet the provisions of paragraph 8.33; and

---

Diagram 25   **Protected shafts**

See paras 8.30-8.32

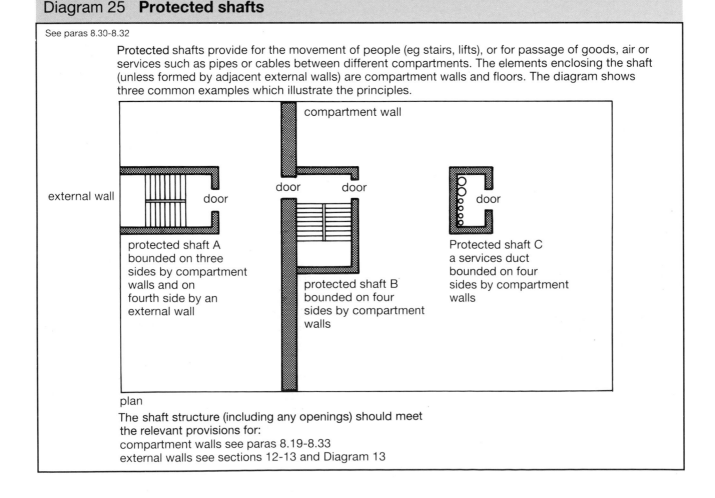

Protected shafts provide for the movement of people (eg stairs, lifts), or for passage of goods, air or services such as pipes or cables between different compartments. The elements enclosing the shaft (unless formed by adjacent external walls) are compartment walls and floors. The diagram shows three common examples which illustrate the principles.

compartment wall

external wall

door

door   door

door

protected shaft A bounded on three sides by compartment walls and on fourth side by an external wall

protected shaft B bounded on four sides by compartment walls

Protected shaft C a services duct bounded on four sides by compartment walls

plan

The shaft structure (including any openings) should meet the relevant provisions for:
compartment walls see paras 8.19-8.33
external walls see sections 12-13 and Diagram 13

---

c. satisfy the provisions about their ventilation and the treatment of openings in paragraphs 8.36 et seq.

Glazed screens to protected shafts

8.33 If the conditions given below and described in Diagram 26 are satisfied, a glazed screen may be incorporated in the enclosure to a protected shaft between a stair and a lobby or corridor which is entered from the stair. The conditions to be satisfied are:

a. the standard of fire resistance for the stair enclosure is not more than 60 minutes; and

b. the protected shaft is not a firefighting shaft

c. the glazed screen has at least 30 minutes fire resistance, in terms of integrity

d. the lobby or corridor is enclosed to at least a 30 minute standard.

8.34 Where the measures in Diagram 26 to protect the lobby or corridor, are not provided, the guidance in Appendix A, Table A4, on the limits on areas of uninsulated glazing apply.

Pipes for oil or gas in protected shafts

8.35 If a protected shaft contains a stair and/or a lift, it should not also contain a pipe conveying oil (other than in the mechanism of a hydraulic lift) or contain a ventilating duct (other than a duct provided for the purposes for pressurizing the stairway to keep it smoke-free). Any pipe carrying natural gas in such a shaft should be of screwed steel or of all welded steel construction, installed in accordance with the Gas Safety Regulations SI 1972, No 1178, and Gas Safety (Installation & use) Regulations 1984 as amended 1990.

Ventilation of protected shafts conveying gas

8.36 A protected shaft conveying piped flammable gas should be adequately ventilated direct to the outside air by ventilation openings at high and low level in the shaft.

Openings into protected shafts

8.37 Generally an external wall of a protected shaft does not need to have fire resistance. However there are some provisions for fire resistance of external walls of firefighting shafts in section 2 of BS5588: Part 5, which is the relevant guidance called up by paragraph 17.11. Openings in other parts of the enclosure to a protected shaft should be limited as follows.

a. Where part of the enclosure to a protected shaft is a wall common to two or more buildings, only the following openings should be made in that wall:

i. a door which is needed to provide a means of escape in case of fire and which has the same fire resistance as that required for the wall (see Appendix B, Table B1) and is fitted in

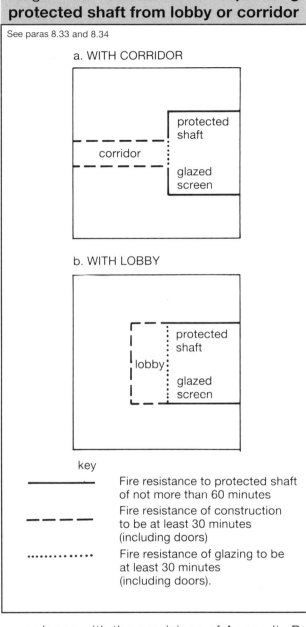

Diagram 26 **Glazed screen separating protected shaft from lobby or corridor**

See paras 8.33 and 8.34

a. WITH CORRIDOR

corridor
protected shaft
glazed screen

b. WITH LOBBY

lobby
protected shaft
glazed screen

key

———— Fire resistance to protected shaft of not more than 60 minutes

– – – – Fire resistance of construction to be at least 30 minutes (including doors)

·············· Fire resistance of glazing to be at least 30 minutes (including doors).

accordance with the provisions of Appendix B; and

ii. the passage of a pipe which meets the provisions in Section 10.

b. Other parts of the enclosure (other than an external wall) should only have openings for:

i. doors which have the appropriate fire resistance given in Appendix B, Table B1, and are fitted in accordance with the provisions of Appendix B; and

ii. the passage of pipes which meet the provisions in Section 10; and

iii. inlets to, outlets from and openings for a ventilation duct, (if the shaft contains or serves as a ventilating duct) which meet the provisions in Section 10; and

iv. the passage of lift cables into a lift machine room (if the shaft contains a lift). If the machine room is at the bottom of the shaft, the openings should be as small as practicable.

Section 9

CONCEALED SPACES (CAVITIES)

Introduction

9.1 Concealed spaces or cavities in the construction of a building provide a ready route for smoke and flame spread. This is particularly so in the case of voids above other spaces in a building, eg above a suspended ceiling or in a roof space. As any spread is concealed, it presents a greater danger than would a more obvious weakness in the fabric of the building. Provisions are made to restrict this by interrupting cavities which could form a pathway around a barrier to fire, and by sub-dividing extensive cavities.

Note on cavities in rain screen cladding and the like: Cavities within an external wall are referred to in this Section, including the drained and ventilated cavities behind the outer cladding in "rain screen" external wall construction. There are also provisions in paragraphs 12.6 and 12.7 about the construction of external walls which have a bearing on overcladding and rainscreen construction.

Provision of cavity barriers

9.2 Provisions for cavity barriers are set out in Table 13 against specified locations and purpose groups.

9.3 Table 14 lays down maximum dimensions for undivided concealed spaces.

9.4 Diagram 27 illustrates the need for cavity barriers at the intersection of fire resisting construction and elements containing a concealed space.

9.5 As compartment walls should be carried up full storey height, to a compartment floor or to the roof as appropriate, see paragraph 8.19, it is not appropriate to complete a line of compartmentation by fitting cavity barriers above them. The fire resistance standards for cavity barriers are lower than for a compartment wall, and it is important to continue the compartment wall through the cavity to maintain the standard of fire resistance.

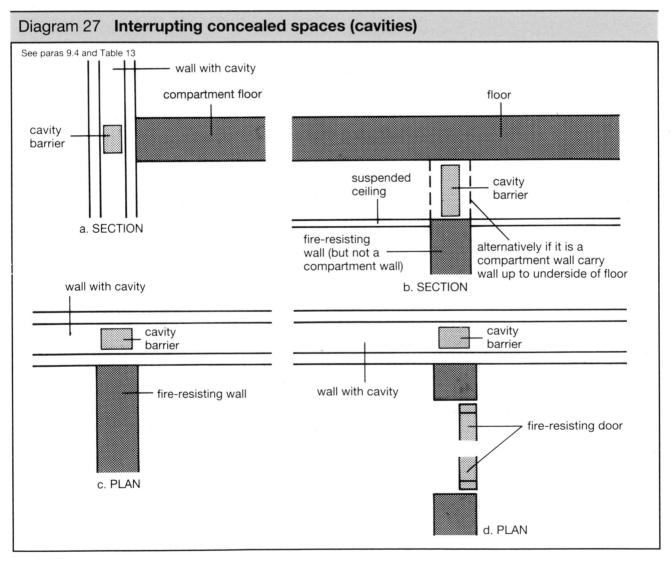

Diagram 27 **Interrupting concealed spaces (cavities)**

Construction and fixings for cavity barriers

9.6 Every cavity barrier should be constructed to provide at least 30 minutes fire resistance (see Appendix A, Table A1, item 16), except for a cavity barrier in a stud wall or partition which may be formed of:-

a. steel at least 0.5 mm thick; or

b. timber at least 38 mm thick; or

c. polythene sleeved mineral wool, or mineral wool slab, in either case under compression when installed in the cavity; or

d. calcium silicate, cement based or gypsum based boards at least 12.5mm thick.

9.7 A cavity barrier may be formed by any construction provided for another purpose if it meets the provisions for cavity barriers.

9.8 Cavity barriers should be tightly fitted to rigid construction and mechanically fixed in position wherever possible. Where this is not possible (for example, in the case of a junction with slates, tiles, corrugated sheeting or similar materials) the junction should be fire-stopped. Provisions for fire stopping are set out in Section 10.

9.9 Cavity barriers should also be fixed so that their performance is unlikely to be made ineffective by:

a. movement of the building due to subsidence, shrinkage or temperature change, and movement of the external envelope due to wind; and

b. collapse in a fire of any services penetrating them; and

c. failure in a fire of their fixings; and

d. failure in a fire of any material or construction which they abut. For example, if a suspended ceiling is continued over the top of a fire-resisting wall or partition, and direct connection is made between the ceiling and the cavity barrier above the line of the wall or partition, premature failure of the cavity barrier can occur when the ceiling collapses. However, this does not arise if the ceiling is designed to provide fire protection of 30 minutes or more.

Maximum dimensions of concealed spaces

9.10 With the exceptions given in paragraphs 9.11 to 9.13, extensive concealed spaces should be sub- divided to comply with the dimensions in Table 14.

9.11 The provisions in Table 14 do not apply to any cavity described below:

a. in a wall which should be fire-resisting only because it is loadbearing;

b. in a masonry or concrete external cavity wall shown in Diagram 28;

c. in any floor or roof cavity above a fire resisting ceiling, as shown in Diagram 31 and which extends throughout the building or compartment, subject to a 30m limit on the extent of the cavity:

d. below a floor next to the ground or oversite concrete, if the cavity is less than 1m in height or if the cavity is not normally accessible by persons, unless there are openings in the floor such that it is possible for combustibles to accumulate in the cavity (in which case cavity barriers should be provided, and access should be provided to the cavity for cleaning);

e. formed behind the external skin in rain-screen external wall construction, or by over-cladding an existing masonry (or concrete) external wall, or an existing concrete roof, provided that the cavity does not contain combustible insulation, and the provisions of Table 13 item 9 are observed; and

f. between double-skinned corrugated or profiled insulated roof sheeting, if the sheeting is a material of limited combustibility and both surfaces of the insulating layer have a surface spread of flame of at least Class 0 or 1 (see Appendix A) and make contact with inner and outer skins of cladding (see Diagram 32).

9.12 Where any room under a ceiling cavity exceeds the dimensions given in Table 14, cavity barriers need only be provided on the line of the enclosing walls/partitions of that room, subject to the cavity barriers being no more than 40m apart

9.13 Where the concealed space is over an undivided area which exceeds 40m (in both directions on plan) there is no limit to the size of the cavity if:

a. the room and the cavity together are compartmented from the rest of the building;

b. an automatic fire detection and alarm system is fitted in the building

c. if the cavity is used as a plenum the recommendations about recirculating air distribution systems in BS 5588: Part 9 are followed

d. the surface of the ceiling exposed in the cavity is Class 0 and the supports and fixings in the cavity are of non-combustible construction;

e. the flame spread rating of any pipe insulation system is Class 1;

f. any electrical wiring in the void is laid in metal trays, or in metal conduit; and

g. any other materials in the cavity are of limited combustibility.

Openings in cavity barriers

9.14 Any openings in a cavity barrier should be limited to those for:

a. doors which have at least 30 minutes fire resistance (see Appendix B, Table B1, item 8(a)) and are fitted in accordance with the provisions of Appendix B;

b. the passage of pipes which meet the provisions in Section 10;

c. the passage of cables or conduits containing one or more cables;

d. openings fitted with a suitably mounted automatic fire shutter; and

e. ducts which (unless they are fire-resisting) are fitted with a suitably mounted automatic fire shutter where they pass through the cavity barrier.

Table 13 Provision of cavity barriers

Cavity barriers to be provided:	Purpose group to which the provision applies(3)			
	1b & c dwelling houses	1a Flat or maisonette	2 Other residential and institutional	3-7 Office, shop & commercial, assembly & recreation, industrial, storage & other non-residential
1. At the junction between an external cavity wall, which does not comply with Diagram 28, and a compartment wall that separates buildings; and at the top of such an external cavity wall.	x	x	x	x
2. Above the enclosures to a protected stairway in a house of three or more storeys (see Diagram 29a). (1)	x	-	-	-
3. At the junction between an external cavity wall which does not comply with Diagram 28, and every compartment floor and compartment wall.	-	x	x	x
4. At the junction between a cavity wall which does not comply with Diagram 28 and every compartment floor, compartment wall, or other wall or door assembly which forms a fire resisting barrier.	-	x	x	x
5. In a protected escape route, above any fire resisting construction which is not carried full storey height, or (in the case of a top storey) to the underside of the roof covering.(1)	-	x	x	x
6. Above any bedroom partitions which are not carried full storey height, or (in the case of the top storey) to the underside of the roof covering.(1)	-	-	x	-
7. Above any corridor enclosures which are not carried full storey height, or (in the case of the top storey) to the underside of the roof covering, where the corridor (which is not a protected corridor) should be sub-divided to prevent fire or smoke affecting two alternative escape routes simultaneously (see paragraph 3.21 & Diagram 30).(2)	-	-	x	x
8. To sub-divide any cavity (including any roof space) so that the distance between cavity barriers does not exceed the dimensions given in Table 14.	-	-	x	x
9. Within the void behind the external face of rainscreen cladding at every floor level, and on the line of compartment walls abutting the external wall, of buildings which have a floor more than 20m above ground level.	-	x	x	-

Key x provision applies
  -   provision does not apply

Notes
1.   The provisions in items 2,5 and 6 do not apply where the cavity is enclosed on the lower side by a fire resisting ceiling (as shown in Diagram 31) which extends throughout the building, compartment or separated part.

2.   The provision of item 7 does not apply where the storey is sub-divided by fire resisting construction carried full storey height and passing through the line of sub-division of the corridor (see Diagram 30), or where the cavity is enclosed on the lower side as described in Note 1.

3.   The classification of purpose groups is set out in Appendix D, Table D1.

Table 14 Maximum dimensions of cavities in non-domestic buildings (purpose groups 2-7)

Location of cavity	Class of surface exposed in cavity (excluding surface of any pipe, cable or conduit, or insulation to any pipe)	Maximum dimension in any direction (m)
Between a roof and a ceiling	Any	20
Any other cavity	Class 0 or Class 1	20
	Class other than Class 0 or 1	10

Note: Exceptions to these provisions are given in paragraphs 9.11 - 9.13

Diagram 28 Cavity walls excluded from provisions for cavity barriers

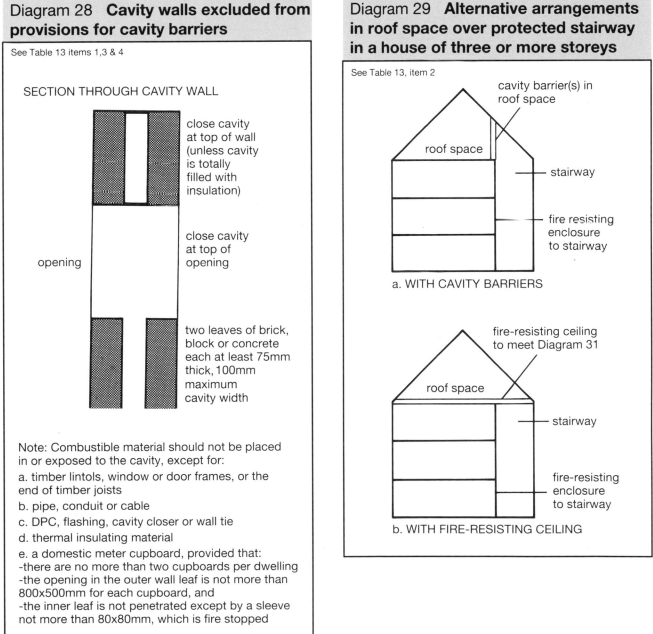

See Table 13 items 1,3 & 4

SECTION THROUGH CAVITY WALL

close cavity at top of wall (unless cavity is totally filled with insulation)

opening

close cavity at top of opening

two leaves of brick, block or concrete each at least 75mm thick, 100mm maximum cavity width

Note: Combustible material should not be placed in or exposed to the cavity, except for:

a. timber lintols, window or door frames, or the end of timber joists

b. pipe, conduit or cable

c. DPC, flashing, cavity closer or wall tie

d. thermal insulating material

e. a domestic meter cupboard, provided that:
-there are no more than two cupboards per dwelling
-the opening in the outer wall leaf is not more than 800x500mm for each cupboard, and
-the inner leaf is not penetrated except by a sleeve not more than 80x80mm, which is fire stopped

Diagram 29 Alternative arrangements in roof space over protected stairway in a house of three or more storeys

See Table 13, item 2

cavity barrier(s) in roof space

roof space

stairway

fire resisting enclosure to stairway

a. WITH CAVITY BARRIERS

fire-resisting ceiling to meet Diagram 31

roof space

stairway

fire-resisting enclosure to stairway

b. WITH FIRE-RESISTING CEILING

Diagram 30 **Corridor enclosure alternatives**

See Table 13 item 7 & note 2 & paragraph 3.21

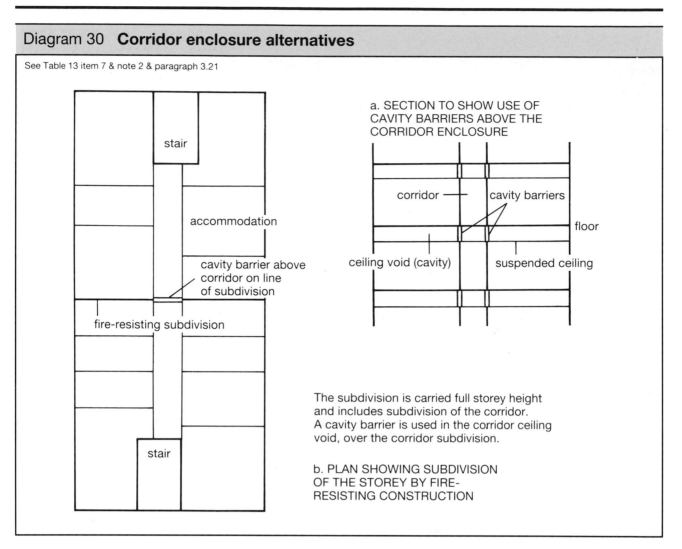

a. SECTION TO SHOW USE OF CAVITY BARRIERS ABOVE THE CORRIDOR ENCLOSURE

corridor — cavity barriers

floor

ceiling void (cavity)   suspended ceiling

stair

accommodation

cavity barrier above corridor on line of subdivision

fire-resisting subdivision

stair

The subdivision is carried full storey height and includes subdivision of the corridor. A cavity barrier is used in the corridor ceiling void, over the corridor subdivision.

b. PLAN SHOWING SUBDIVISION OF THE STOREY BY FIRE-RESISTING CONSTRUCTION

Diagram 31 **Fire-resisting ceiling below concealed space**

See para 9.11c & Table 13 note 1

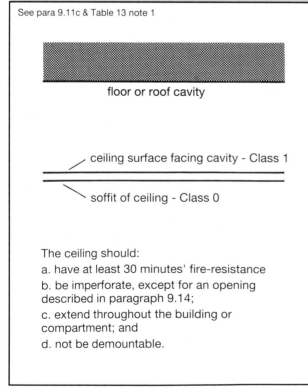

floor or roof cavity

ceiling surface facing cavity - Class 1

soffit of ceiling - Class 0

The ceiling should:

a. have at least 30 minutes' fire-resistance

b. be imperforate, except for an opening described in paragraph 9.14;

c. extend throughout the building or compartment; and

d. not be demountable.

Diagram 32 **Provisions for cavity barriers in double skinned insulated roof sheeting**

See para 9.11f

a. ACCEPTABLE WITHOUT CAVITY BARRIERS

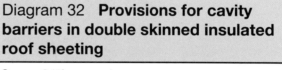

The insulation should make contact with both skins of sheeting.

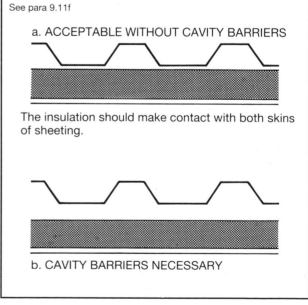

b. CAVITY BARRIERS NECESSARY

Section 10

PROTECTION OF OPENINGS AND FIRE STOPPING

Introduction

10.1 Sections 8 and 9 make provisions for fire separating elements, and set out the circumstances in which there may be openings in them. This section deals with the protection of openings in such elements.

10.2 If an element that is intended to provide fire separation (and therefore has fire resistance in terms of integrity and insulation) is to be effective, then every joint, or imperfection of fit, or opening to allow services to pass through the element, should be adequately protected by sealing or fire-stopping so that the fire resistance of the element is not impaired.

10.3 The measures in this section are intended to delay the passage of fire. They generally have the additional benefit of retarding smoke spread, but the test specified in Appendix A for integrity does not stipulate criteria for the passage of smoke as such.

10.4 Detailed guidance on door openings and fire doors is given in Appendix B.

Table 15 Maximum nominal internal diameter of pipes passing through a compartment wall/floor (see paragraph 10.5 et seq)

Situation	Pipe material and maximum nominal internal diameter (mm)		
	(a) Non-combustible material(1)	(b) Lead, aluminium aluminium alloy, PVC(2)fibre-cement	(c) Any other material
1. Structure (but not a wall separating buildings) enclosing a protected shaft which is not a stairway or a lift shaft.	160	110	40
2. Wall separating dwellinghouses, or compartment wall or compartment floor between flats.	160	160 (stack pipe)(3) 110 (branch pipe)(3)	40
3. Any other situation	160	40	40

Notes
1. A non-combustible material (such as cast iron or steel) which if exposed to a temperature of 800°C, will not soften or fracture to the extent that flame or hot gas will pass through the wall of the pipe.

2. PVC pipes complying with BS 4514: 1983 and PVC pipes complying with BS 5255: 1989.

3. These diameters are only in relation to pipes forming part of an above-ground drainage system and enclosed as shown in Diagram 34. In other cases the maximum diameters against situation 3 apply.

Openings for pipes

10.5 Pipes which pass through a compartment wall or compartment floor (unless the pipe is in a protected shaft), or through a cavity barrier, should meet the appropriate provisions in alternatives A, B or C below.

Alternative A: Proprietary seals (any pipe diameter)

10.6 Provide a proprietary sealing system which has been shown by test to maintain the fire resistance of the wall, floor or cavity barrier.

Alternative B: pipes with a restricted diameter

10.7 Where a proprietary sealing system is not used, fire-stopping may be used around the pipe, keeping the opening as small as possible. The nominal internal diameter of the pipe should not be more than the relevant dimension given in Table 15.

10.8 The diameters given in Table 15 for pipes of specification (b) used in situation (2) assume that the pipes are part of an above-ground drainage system and are enclosed as shown in Diagram 34. If they are not, the smaller diameter given in situation (3) should be used.

Alternative C: Sleeving

10.9 A pipe of lead, aluminium, aluminium alloy, fibre-cement or PVC, with a maximum nominal internal diameter of 160mm, may be used with a sleeving of non-combustible pipe as shown in Diagram 33. The specification for non-combustible and PVC pipes is given in the notes to Table 15.

Diagram 33 Pipes penetrating structure

See para 10.9, alternative method c

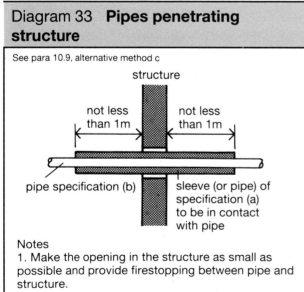

structure

not less than 1m   not less than 1m

pipe specification (b)   sleeve (or pipe) of specification (a) to be in contact with pipe

Notes
1. Make the opening in the structure as small as possible and provide firestopping between pipe and structure.
2. See Table 15 for materials specification.

Ventilating ducts

10.10 BS 5588: Part 9 sets out alternative ways in which the integrity of compartments may be maintained where ventilation and air conditioning ducts penetrate fire separating elements. The alternatives are equally acceptable, and the recommendations of that code should be followed where air handling ducts pass from one compartment to another.

Flues, etc

10.11 If a flue, or duct containing flues or appliance ventilation duct(s), passes through a compartment wall or compartment floor, or is built into a compartment wall, each wall of the flue or duct should have a fire resistance of at least half that of the wall or floor in order to prevent the by-passing of the compartmentation (see Diagram 35).

Fire-stopping

10.12 In addition to any other provisions in this document for fire-stopping:

a.   joints between elements which serve as a barrier to the passage of fire should be fire-stopped; and

b.   all openings for pipes, ducts, conduits or cables to pass through any part of an element which serves as a barrier to the passage of fire should be:

i.   kept as few in number as possible, and

ii.   kept as small as practicable, and

iii.   fire-stopped (which in the case of a pipe or duct, should allow thermal movement).

10.13 To prevent displacement, materials used for fire-stopping should be reinforced with (or supported by) materials of limited combustibility in the following circumstances:

a.   in all cases where the unsupported span is greater than 100mm, and

b.   in any other case where non-rigid materials are used (unless they have been shown to be satisfactory by test).

10.14 Proprietary fire-stopping and sealing systems, (including those designed for service penetrations) which have been shown by test to maintain the fire resistance of the wall or other element, are available and may be used.

Other fire-stopping materials include:

*cement mortar,
*gypsum based plaster,
*cement or gypsum based vermiculite/perlite mixes,
*glass fibre, crushed rock, blast furnace slag or ceramic based products (with or without resin binders), and
* intumescent mastics.

These may be used in situations appropriate to the particular material. Not all of them will be suitable in every situation.

Diagram 34 Enclosure for drainage or water supply pipes

See para 10.8 & Table 15

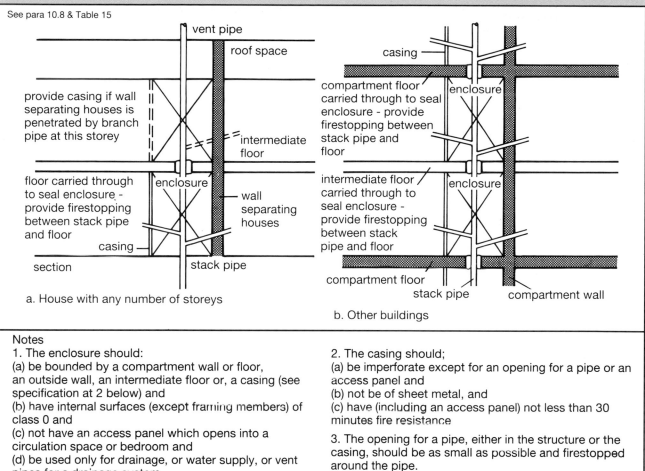

a. House with any number of storeys

b. Other buildings

Notes

1. The enclosure should:
(a) be bounded by a compartment wall or floor, an outside wall, an intermediate floor or, a casing (see specification at 2 below) and
(b) have internal surfaces (except framing members) of class 0 and
(c) not have an access panel which opens into a circulation space or bedroom and
(d) be used only for drainage, or water supply, or vent pipes for a drainage system.

2. The casing should;
(a) be imperforate except for an opening for a pipe or an access panel and
(b) not be of sheet metal, and
(c) have (including an access panel) not less than 30 minutes fire resistance

3. The opening for a pipe, either in the structure or the casing, should be as small as possible and firestopped around the pipe.

Diagram 35 Flues and compartment walls or floors

See para 10.11

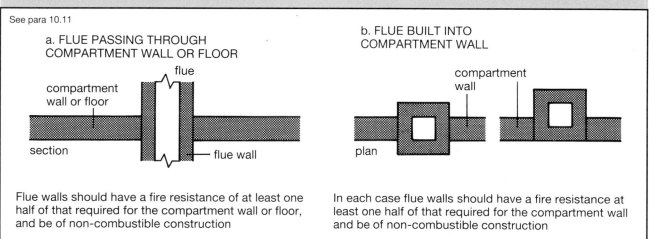

a. FLUE PASSING THROUGH COMPARTMENT WALL OR FLOOR

Flue walls should have a fire resistance of at least one half of that required for the compartment wall or floor, and be of non-combustible construction

b. FLUE BUILT INTO COMPARTMENT WALL

In each case flue walls should have a fire resistance at least one half of that required for the compartment wall and be of non-combustible construction

Section 11

SPECIAL PROVISIONS FOR CAR PARKS AND SHOPPING COMPLEXES

Introduction

11.1 This section describes additional considerations which apply to the design and construction of car parks and shopping complexes.

Car Parks

General principles

11.2 Buildings or parts of buildings used as parking for cars and other light vehicles are unlike other buildings in certain respects which merit some departures from the usual measures to restrict fire spread within buildings.

a. The fire load is well defined and not particularly high.

b. There is some evidence that fire spread is not likely to occur between one vehicle and another, where the car park is well ventilated and there is a correspondingly low probability of fire spread from one storey to another. Ventilation is the important factor, and as heat and smoke cannot be dissipated so readily from a car park that is not open -sided fewer concessions are made. The following guidance is concerned with three ventilation methods: open sided (high level of natural ventilation), natural ventilation and mechanical ventilation.

Provisions common to all car park buildings

11.3 The relevant provisions of the guidance on requirements B1 and B5 will apply, but in addition all materials used in the construction of the building, compartment or separated part should be non-combustible, except for:

a   any surface finish applied:-

i.   to a floor or roof of the car park, or

ii.   within any adjoining building, compartment or separated part to the structure enclosing the car park, if the finish meets all relevant aspects of the guidance on requirements B2 and B4.

b.   any fire door; and

c.   any attendant's kiosk not exceeding 15m^2 in area.

Open sided car parks

11.4 If the building, or separated part containing the car park, complies with the following provisions (in addition to those in paragraph 11.3) it may be regarded as an open-sided car park for the purposes of fire

resistance assessment in Appendix A, Table A2, and it may be regarded as a small building or compartment, for the purposes of space separation in Table 16. The provisions are that:

a.   there should not be any basement storeys;

b.   each storey should be naturally ventilated by permanent openings at each car parking level, having an aggregate vent area not less than 5% of the floor area at that level, of which at least half should be in two opposing walls;

c.   if the building is also used for any other purpose, the part forming the car park is a separated part.

Car parks which are not open sided

11.5 Where car parks do not have the standard of ventilation set out in 11.4(b), they are not regarded as open-sided and a different standard of fire resistance is necessary (the relevant provisions are given in Appendix A, Table A2).

Such car parks still require some ventilation, which may be by natural or mechanical means, as described in 11.6 or 11.7 below. The provisions of 11.3 apply to all car park buildings, whatever standard of ventilation is provided.

Natural ventilation

11.6 Where car parks that are not open-sided are provided with some, more limited, natural ventilation, each storey should be ventilated by permanent openings at each car parking level, having an aggregate vent area not less than 2.5% of the floor area at that level, of which at least half should be in two opposing walls. Smoke vents at ceiling level may be used as an alternative to the provision of permanent openings in the walls. They should have an aggregate area of permanent opening totalling not less than 2.5% of the floor area and be arranged to provide a through draught.

Mechanical ventilation

11.7 In most basement car parks, and in enclosed car parks, it may not be possible to obtain the minimum standard of natural ventilation openings set out in paragraph 11.6 above. In such cases a system of mechanical ventilation should be provided as follows:

a.   the system should be independent of any other ventilating system and be designed to operate at 6 air changes per hour for normal petrol vapour extraction, and at 10 air changes per hour in a fire condition;

b.   the system should be designed to run in two parts, each part capable of extracting 50% of the rates set out in (a) above, and designed so that each part may operate singly or simultaneously;

c. each part of the system should have an independent power supply which would operate in the event of failure of the main supply;

d. extract points should be arranged so that 50% of the outlets are at high level, and 50% at low level; and

e. The fans should be rated to run at 300°C for a minimum of 60 mins, and the ductwork and fixings should be constructed of materials having a melting point not less than 800°C.

Shopping Complexes

11.8 Whilst the provisions in this document about shops should generally be capable of application in cases where a shop is contained in a single separate building, the provisions may not be appropriate where a shop forms part of a complex. These may include covered malls providing access to a number of shops and common servicing areas. In particular the provisions about maximum compartment size may be difficult to meet bearing in mind that it would generally not be practical to compartment a shop from a mall serving it. To a lesser extent the provisions about fire resistance, walls separating shop units, surfaces and boundary distances may pose problems.

11.9 To ensure a satisfactory standard of fire safety in shopping complexes, alternative measures and additional compensatory features to those set out in this document are appropriate. Such features are set out in sections five and six of BS 5588: Part 10, and the relevant recommendations of those sections should be followed.

The Requirement

This Approved Document which takes effect on
1 June 1992 deals with the following
Requirement from Part B of Schedule 1 to the
Building Regulations 1991.

Requirement	Limits on application

External fire spread

B4. (1) The external walls of the building shall resist the spread of fire over the walls and from one building to another, having regard to the height, use and position of the building.

(2) The roof of the building shall resist the spread of fire over the roof and from one building to another, having regard to the use and position of the building.

Guidance

Performance

In the Secretary of State's view the requirements of B4 will be met:

a. if the external walls are constructed so that the risk of ignition from an external source, and the spread of fire over their surfaces, is restricted by making provision for them to have low rates of heat release;

b. if the amount of unprotected area in the side of the building is restricted so as to limit the amount of thermal radiation that can pass through the wall, taking the distance between the wall and the boundary into account, and;

c. if the roof is constructed so that the risk of spread of flame and/or fire penetration from an external fire source is restricted.

In each case so as to limit the risk of a fire spreading from the building to a building beyond the boundary, or vice versa.

The extent to which this is necessary is dependent on the use of the building, its distance from the boundary and, in some cases, its height.

Introduction

External walls

* **0.49** The construction of external walls and the separation between buildings to prevent external fire spread are closely related.

The chances of fire spreading across an open space between buildings, and the consequences if it does, depend on:

a. the size and intensity of the fire in the building concerned

b. the distance between the buildings,

c. the fire protection given by their facing sides, and

d. the risk presented to people in the other building(s)

0.50 Provisions are made in Section 12 for the fire resistance of external walls and to limit the susceptibility of the external surface of walls to ignition and to fire spread.

0.51 Provisions are made in Section 13 to limit the extent of openings and other unprotected areas in external walls in order to reduce the risk of fire spread by radiation.

Roofs

0.52 Provisions are made in Section 14 for reducing the risk of fire spread between roofs and over the surfaces of roofs.

* Introductory paragraphs 0.46 - 0.48 are on page 51

Section 12

CONSTRUCTION OF EXTERNAL WALLS

Introduction

12.1 Provisions are made in this section for the external walls of the building to have sufficient fire resistance to prevent fire spread across the relevant boundary. The provisions are closely linked with those for space separation in Section 13 (following) which sets out limits on the amount of unprotected area of wall. As the limits depend on the distance of the wall from the relevant boundary, it is possible for some or all of the walls, to have no fire resistance, except for any parts which are loadbearing (see paragraph 0.47).

External walls are elements of structure and the relevant period of fire resistance (specified in Appendix A) depends on the use, height and size of the building concerned. if the wall is 1m or more from the relevant boundary a reduced standard of fire resistance is accepted in most cases (no insulation criterion is applied), and the wall only needs fire resistance from the inside.

12.2 Provisions are also made to restrict the combustibility of external walls of buildings that are less than 1m from the relevant boundary, and, irrespective of boundary distance, the external walls of high buildings and those of the assembly and recreation purpose groups. This is in order to reduce the surface's susceptibility to ignition from an external source, and to reduce the danger from fire spread up the external face of the building.

In the guidance to Requirement B3, provisions are made in Section 7 for internal and external loadbearing walls to maintain their loadbearing function in the event of fire.

Fire resistance standard

12.3 The external walls of the building should have the appropriate fire resistance given in Table A1, Appendix A, unless they form an unprotected area under the provisions of Section 13.

Portal frames

12.4 Portal frames are often used in single storey industrial and commercial buildings where there may be no need for fire resistance of the structure (requirement B3). However, where a portal framed building is near a relevant boundary the external wall near the boundary may need fire resistance to restrict the spread of fire between buildings.

It is generally accepted that a portal frame acts as a single structural element because of the moment-resisting connections used, especially at the column/rafter joints. Thus in cases where the external wall of the building cannot be wholly unprotected, the rafter members of the frame, as well as the column members, may need to be fire protected.

Following an investigation of the behaviour of steel portal frames in fire, it is considered technically and economically feasible to design the foundation and its connection to the portal frame so that it would transmit the overturning moment caused by the collapse, in a fire, of unprotected rafters, purlins and some roof cladding while allowing the external wall to continue to perform its structural function. The design method for this is set out in *Fire and steel construction: The Behaviour of Steel Portal frames in Boundary Conditions,* 1990 (2nd edition), which is available from the Steel Construction Institute, Silwood Park, Ascot, Berks, SL5 7QN. This publication offers guidance on many aspects of portal frames, including multi-storey types.

Normally, portal frames of reinforced concrete can support external walls requiring a similar degree of fire resistance without specific provision at the base to resist overturning.

External surfaces

12.5 The external surfaces of walls should meet the provisions in Diagram 36. However, the total amount of combustible material may be limited in practice by the provisions for space separation in Section 13. (See paragraph 13.7 et seq.)

12.6 In the case of the outer cladding of a wall of 'rainscreen' construction (with a drained and ventilated cavity) the surface of the outer cladding which faces the cavity should also meet the provisions of Diagram 36.

External wall construction

12.7 The external envelope of a building should not provide a medium for fire spread if it is likely to be a risk to health or safety. The use of combustible materials for cladding framework, or of combustible thermal insulation as an overcladding or in ventilated cavities, may present such a risk in tall buildings, even though the provisions for external surfaces in Diagram 36 may have been satisfied.

In a building with a storey at more than 20m above ground level, insulation material used in the external wall construction should be of limited combustibility (see Appendix A). This restriction does not apply to masonry cavity wall construction which complies with Diagram 28 in Section 9.

Advice on the use of thermal insulation material is given in the Building Research Establishment Report "Fire performance of external thermal insulation for walls of multi-storey buildings (BR 135, 1988)".

Diagram 36 Provisions for external surfaces of walls

See para 12.5 and 12.6

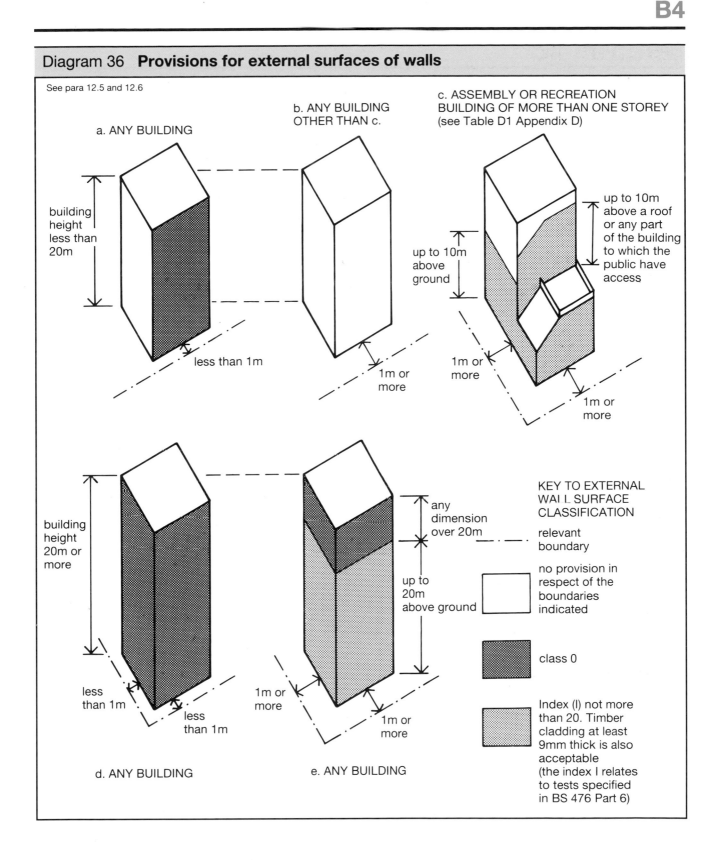

a. ANY BUILDING

building height less than 20m

less than 1m

b. ANY BUILDING OTHER THAN c.

up to 10m above ground

1m or more

c. ASSEMBLY OR RECREATION BUILDING OF MORE THAN ONE STOREY (see Table D1 Appendix D)

up to 10m above a roof or any part of the building to which the public have access

1m or more

1m or more

d. ANY BUILDING

building height 20m or more

less than 1m

less than 1m

e. ANY BUILDING

any dimension over 20m

up to 20m above ground

1m or more

1m or more

KEY TO EXTERNAL WALL SURFACE CLASSIFICATION

—·—·— relevant boundary

no provision in respect of the boundaries indicated

class 0

Index (I) not more than 20. Timber cladding at least 9mm thick is also acceptable (the index I relates to tests specified in BS 476 Part 6)

Section 13

SPACE SEPARATION

Introduction

13.1 The provisions in this section are based on a number of assumptions, and whilst some of these may differ from the circumstances of a particular case, together they enable a reasonable standard of space separation to be specified. The provisions limit the extent of unprotected areas in the sides of a building (such as openings and areas with a combustible surface) which will not give adequate protection against the external spread of fire from one building to another.

13.2 The assumptions are:

a.   that the size of a fire will depend on the compartmentation of the building, so that a fire may involve a complete compartment, but will not spread to other compartments;

b.   that the intensity of the fire is related to the use of the building (ie purpose group), but that it can be moderated by a sprinkler system;

c.   that Residential, and Assembly and Recreation purpose groups represent a greater life risk than other uses;

d.   that apart from Residential, and Assembly and Recreation purpose groups, the spread of fire between buildings on the same site represents a low risk to life and can be discounted;

e.   that there is a building on the far side of the boundary that has a similar elevation to the one in question, and that it is at the same distance from the common boundary; and

f.   that the amount of radiation that passes through any part of the external wall that has fire resistance may be discounted.

13.3 Where a reduced separation distance is desired (or an increased amount of unprotected area) it may be advantageous to construct compartments of a smaller size.

Boundaries

13.4 The use of the distance to a boundary rather than to another building, in measuring the separation distance, makes it possible to calculate the allowable proportion of unprotected areas, regardless of whether there is a building on an adjoining site, and regardless of the site of that building, and the extent of any unprotected areas that it might have .

A wall is treated as facing a boundary if it makes an angle with it of 80° or less (see Diagram 37).

Usually only the distance to the actual boundary of the site needs to be considered. But in some circumstances, when the site boundary adjoins a space where further development is unlikely, such as a road, then part of the adjoining space may be included as falling within the relevant boundary for the purposes of this section. The meaning of the term boundary is explained in Diagram 37.

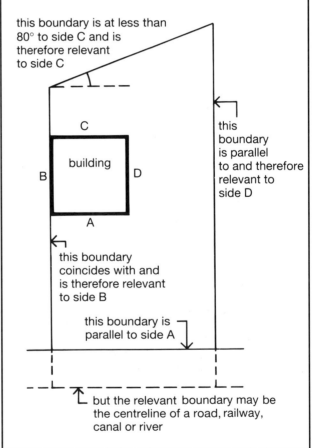

Diagram 37   **Relevant boundary**

See para 13.4

This diagram sets out the rules that apply in respect of a boundary for it to be considered as a relevant boundary.

For a boundary to be relevant it should:
a. coinside with, or
b. be parallel to, or
c. be at an angle of not more than 80° to the side of the building

this boundary is at less than 80° to side C and is therefore relevant to side C

C

building

B   D

A

this boundary is parallel to and therefore relevant to side D

this boundary coincides with and is therefore relevant to side B

this boundary is parallel to side A

but the relevant boundary may be the centreline of a road, railway, canal or river

Diagram 38 Notional boundary

See para 13.6

This diagram sets out the rules that apply where there is a building of the residential, or assembly and recreational, purpose groups on the same site as another building, so that a notional boundary needs to be assumed between the buildings.

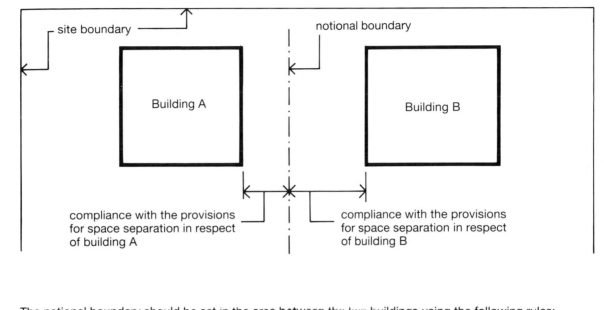

The notional boundary should be set in the area between the two buildings using the following rules:

1. It is only necessary to assume a notional boundary when the buildings are on the same site and either of the buildings, new or existing, is of Residential or Assembly and recreation use.

2. The notional boundary is assumed to exist in the space between the buildings and is positioned so that one of the buildings would comply with the provisions for space separation having regard to the amount of its unprotected area.

In practice, if one of the buildings is existing, the position of the boundary will be set by the space separation factors for that building.

3. The siting of the new building, or the second building if both are new, can then be checked to see that it also complies - using the notional boundary as the relevant boundary for the second building.

Relevant boundaries

13.5 The boundary which a wall faces, whether it is the actual boundary of the site or a notional boundary, is called the relevant boundary. (See Diagrams 37 and 38).

Notional boundaries

13.6 Generally separation distance between buildings on the same site is discounted. In some circumstances the distances to other buildings on the same site need to be considered. This is done by assuming that there is a boundary between those buildings. This assumed boundary is called a notional boundary. A notional boundary is assumed to exist where either or both of the buildings concerned are in the Residential or Assembly and Recreation purpose groups. The appropriate rules are given in Diagram 38.

Unprotected areas

Unprotected areas and fire resistance

13.7 Any part of an external wall which has less fire resistance than the appropriate amount given in Table A2, Appendix A is considered to be an unprotected area.

External walls of protected shafts forming stairways

13.8 Any part of an external wall of a stairway in a protected shaft is excluded from the assessment of unprotected area, but note that there are provisions in the guidance to B1 (diagram 13) and B5 (BS 5588: Part 5: Section 2) about the relationship of external walls for protected stairways to the unprotected areas of other parts of the building.

Status of combustible surface materials as unprotected area

13.9 If an external wall has the appropriate fire resistance, but has a combustible material more than 1mm thick as its external surface, then that wall is counted as an unprotected area amounting to half the actual area of the combustible surface material, see Diagram 39.

Diagram 39 Status of combustible surface material as unprotected area

See para 13.9

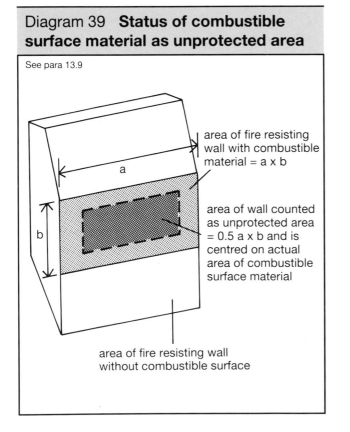

area of fire resisting wall with combustible material = a x b

area of wall counted as unprotected area = 0.5 a x b and is centred on actual area of combustible surface material

area of fire resisting wall without combustible surface

Small unprotected areas

13.10 Small unprotected areas in an otherwise protected area of wall are considered to pose a negligible risk of fire spread, and may be disregarded. Diagram 40 shows the constraints that apply to the placing of such areas in relation to each other and to lines of compartmentation inside the building. These constraints vary according to the size of each unprotected area.

Canopies

13.11 Whilst some canopy structures would be exempt from the application of the Building Regulations by falling within Class VI or Class VII of Schedule 3 to the Regulations (Exempt buildings and works), any which did not meet the criteria for size and boundary distance would not be so exempt.

In such cases, the provisions in this Section about limits of unprotected areas could be onerous.

In view of the high degree of ventilation and heat dissipation achieved by the open sided construction, and provided the canopy is 1m or more from the relevant boundary, the provisions for space separation could reasonably be disregarded. However it would still be subject to limitations on the use of plastics rooflights set out in Table 18.

Large uncompartmented buildings

13.12 Parts of the external wall of an uncompartmented building which are more than 30m above mean ground level, may be disregarded in the assessment of unprotected area.

Diagram 40 Unprotected areas which may be disregarded in assessing the separation distance from the boundary

See para 13.10

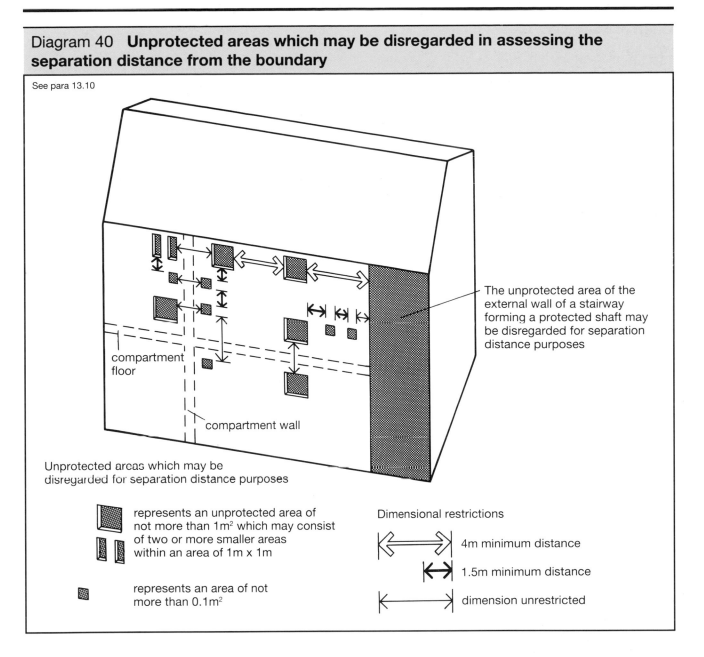

The unprotected area of the external wall of a stairway forming a protected shaft may be disregarded for separation distance purposes

compartment floor

compartment wall

Unprotected areas which may be disregarded for separation distance purposes

represents an unprotected area of not more than 1m² which may consist of two or more smaller areas within an area of 1m x 1m

represents an area of not more than 0.1m²

Dimensional restrictions

4m minimum distance

1.5m minimum distance

dimension unrestricted

External walls within 1m of the relevant boundary

13.13 A wall situated within 1m from any point on the relevant boundary, and including a wall coincident with the boundary, will meet the provisions for space separation if:

a. the only unprotected areas are those shown in Diagram 40 or referred to in paragraph 13.12, and

b. the rest of the wall is fire-resisting from both sides.

External walls 1m or more from the relevant boundary

13.14 A wall situated at least 1m from any point on the relevant boundary will meet the provisions for space separation if:

a. the extent of unprotected area does not exceed that given by one of the methods referred to in paragraph 13.16, and

b. the rest of the wall (if any) is fire-resisting.

Methods for calculating acceptable unprotected area

13.15 Two methods are given in this Approved Document for calculating the acceptable amount of unprotected area in an external wall that is at least 1m from any point on the relevant boundary. (For walls within 1m of the boundary see 13.13 above).

Method 1 may be used for small residential buildings which do not belong to Purpose group 2a (Institutional type premises), and is set out in paragraph 13.19

Method 2 may be used for most buildings or compartments for which Method 1 is not appropriate, and is set out in paragraph 13.20

There are other methods, described in a BRE Report *External fire spread: Building separation and boundary distances*, BRE 1991, which may be used instead of methods 1 and 2.

Basis for calculating acceptable unprotected area

13.16 The basis of Methods 1 and 2 is set out in Fire Research Technical Paper No 5, 1963. This has been reprinted as part of the BRE Report referred to in paragraph 13.15. The aim is to ensure that the building is separated from the boundary by at least half the distance at which the total thermal radiation intensity received from all unprotected areas in the wall would be 12.6 kw/m^2 (in still air), assuming the radiation intensity at each unprotected area is:

a. 84 kw/m^2, if the building is in the Residential, Office or Assembly and Recreation purpose groups, and

b. 168 kw/m^2, if the building is in the Shop and Commercial, Industrial, Storage or Other non-residential purpose groups.

Sprinkler systems

13.17 If a building is fitted throughout with a sprinkler system it is reasonable to assume that the intensity and extent of a fire will be reduced. The sprinkler system should meet the relevant recommendations of BS 5306: Part 2, ie the relevant occupancy rating together with the additional requirements for life safety. In these circumstances the boundary distance may be half that for an otherwise similar, but unsprinklered, building, subject to there being a minimum distance of 1m.

Enclosing rectangle and aggregate notional area methods

13.18 Part 1 of the BRE Report referred to in paragraph 13.15 covers the "Enclosing Rectangle" and "Aggregate Notional Area" methods that were described in Appendix J of the 1985 edition of Approved Document B2/3/4 (which may also be used).

Method 1 - Small Residential

13.19 This method applies only to a building intended to be used as a dwelling house, or for flats or other residential purposes (not Institutional), which is 1m or more from any point on the relevant boundary.

The following rules for determining the maximum unprotected area should be read with Diagram 41.

a. The building should not exceed 3 storeys in height (basements not counted) or be more than 24 m in length.

b. Each side of the building will meet the provisions for space separation if:

i. the distance of the side of the building from the relevant boundary, and

ii. the extent of the unprotected area, are within the limits given in Diagram 41. Note: In calculating the maximum unprotected area, any areas falling within the limits shown in Diagram 40, and referred to in paragraph 13.10 can be disregarded.

c. Any parts of the side of the building in excess of the maximum unprotected area should be fire-resisting.

Diagram 41 Permitted unprotected areas in small residential buildings

Minimum distance (A) between side of building and relevant boundary	Maximum total area of unprotected areas (sq.m.)
1m	5.6
2m	12
3m	18
4m	24
5m	30
6m	no limit

Method 2 - Other buildings or compartments

13.20 This method applies to a building or compartment intended for any use and which is not less than 1m from any point on the relevant boundary. The following rules for determining the maximum unprotected area should be read with Table 16.

a. Except for an open-sided car park in purpose group 7(b) (see paragraph 11.4), the building or compartment should not exceed 10m in height.

Note: for any building or compartment more than 10m in height the methods set out in the BRE Report "External Fire Spread: Building separation and boundary distances" (BRE 1991) can be applied.

b. Each side of the building will meet the provisions for space separation if:

i. the distance of the side of the building from the relevant boundary, and

ii. the extent of unprotected area, are within the appropriate limits given in Table 16.

Note: in calculating the maximum unprotected area, any areas shown in Diagram 40, and referred to in paragraph 13.10, can be disregarded.

c. Any parts of the side of the building in excess of the maximum unprotected area should be fire resisting.

Table 16 Permitted unprotected areas in small buildings or compartments

Minimum distance between side of building and relevant boundary (m)		Maximum total percentage of unprotected area %
Purpose groups		
Residential, Office, Assembly and Recreation	Shop & Commercial Industrial, storage & other Non-residential	
(1)	(2)	(3)
n.a.	1	4
1	2	8
2.5	5	20
5	10	40
7.5	15	60
10	20	80
12.5	25	100

Notes

n.a. = not applicable

a. intermediate values may be obtained by interpolation

b. For buildings which are fitted throughout with an automatic sprinkler system, meeting the relevant recommendations of BS5306: Part 2. the values in columns (1) & (2) may be halved, subject to a minimum distance of 1m being maintained.

c. In the case of open-sided car parks in purpose group 7(b) the distances set out in column (1) may be used instead of those in column (2).

Section 14

ROOF COVERINGS

Introduction
14.1 The provisions in this section limit the use, near a boundary, of roof coverings which will not give adequate protection against the spread of fire over them. The term roof covering is used to describe constructions which may consist of one or more layers of material, but does not refer to the roof structure as a whole. The provisions in this section are principally concerned with the performance of roofs when exposed to fire from the outside.

Other controls on roofs
14.2 There are provisions concerning the fire properties of roofs in three other Sections of this Document. In the guidance to B1 (paragraph 5.3) there are provisions for roofs that are part of a means of escape. In the guidance to B2 (paragraph 6.9), there are provisions for the internal surfaces of rooflights as part of the internal lining of a room or circulation space. In the guidance to B3, there are provisions in Section 7 for roofs which are used as a floor, and in Section 8 for roofs that pass over the top of a compartment wall.

Classification of performance
14.3 The performance of roof coverings is designated by reference to the test methods specified in BS 476: Part 3: 1958, as described in Appendix A. The notional performance of some common roof coverings is given in Table A5 of Appendix A.

Rooflights are controlled on a similar basis, and plastics rooflights, described in paragraph 14.5 and 14.6 may also be used.

Separation distances
14.4 The separation distance is the minimum distance from the roof (or part of the roof) to the relevant boundary, which may be a notional boundary.

Note: The boundary formed by the wall separating a pair of semi-detached houses may be disregarded for the purposes of this section.

Table 17 sets out separation distances according to the type of roof covering and the size and use of the building. There are no restrictions on the use of roof coverings designated AA, AB or AC.

Plastics rooflights
14.5 Table 18 sets out the limitations on the use of plastics rooflights which have at least a Class 3 lower surface, or are constructed of thermoplastic materials with a TP(a) rigid or TP(b) classification (see also Diagram 42). The method of classifying thermoplastic materials is given in Appendix A.

14.6 When used in rooflights, a rigid Thermoplastic sheet product made from polycarbonate or from unplasticised PVC, which achieves a Class 1 rating for surface flame spread when tested to BS 476 Part 7, 1971 or 1987, can be regarded as having an AA designation.

Unwired glass in rooflights
14.7 When used in rooflights, unwired glass at least 4mm thick can be regarded as having an AA designation.

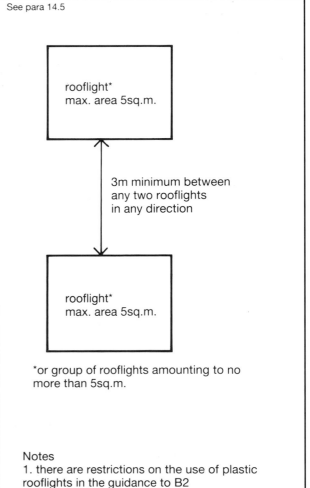

Diagram 42 Limitations on spacing and size of plastics rooflights having a Class 3 or Tp(b) lower surface

See para 14.5

rooflight*
max. area 5sq.m.

3m minimum between any two rooflights in any direction

rooflight*
max. area 5sq.m.

*or group of rooflights amounting to no more than 5sq.m.

Notes
1. there are restrictions on the use of plastic rooflights in the guidance to B2
2. Surrounding roof covering to be a material of limited combustibility for at least 3m distance.

Table 17 Limitations on roof coverings*

Designation of covering of roof or part of roof	Minimum distance from any point on relevant boundary			
	Less than 6m	At least 6m	At least 12m	At least 20m
AA, AB, or AC	●	●	●	●
BA, BB, or BC	○	●	●	●
CA, CB, or CC	○	●(1)	●(2)	●
AD, BD, or CD	○	●(1)	●(2)	●(2)
DA, DB, DC, or DD	○	○	○	●(1)
Thatch or wood shingles, if performance under BS 476: pt 3: 1958 cannot be established	○	●(1)	●(2)	●(2)

Notes:

Separation distance considerations do not apply to roofs of a pair of a pair of semi-detached houses (see 14.4)

* See paragraph 14.7 for limitations on glass, and paragraphs 14.5 and 14.6 and Table 18 for limitations on plastics rooflights.

● Acceptable

○ Not acceptable

(1) Not acceptable on any of the following buildings:
a. Houses in terraces of three or more houses,

b. Industrial, Storage or Other non-residential purpose group buildings of any size,
c. Any other buildings with a cubic capacity of more than 1500m^3

And only acceptable on other buildings if the part of the roof is no more than 3m^2 in area and is at least 1.5m from any similar part, with the roof between the parts covered with a material of limited combustibility.

(2) Not acceptable on any of the buildings listed under a, b or c above.

Table 18 Plastics rooflights: limitations on use and boundary distance

Classification on lower surface (1)	Space which rooflight can serve	Minimum distance from any point on relevant boundary to rooflight with an external surface classification(2) of:		
		TP(a) AD BD CA CB CC CD or TP(b)		DA DB DC DD
1. TP(a) rigid	any space except a protected stairway	6m(3)	6m(5)	20m
2. Class 3 or TP(b)	a. balcony, verandah, carport, covered way or loading bay, which has at least one longer side wholly or permanently open	6m	6m	20m
	b. detached swimming pool			
	c. conservatory, garage or outbuilding, with a maximum floor area of 40m^2			
	d. circulation space(4) (except a protected stairway)	6m(5)	6m(5)	20m(5)
	e. room(4)			

Notes:

na Not applicable.

(1) See also the guidance to B2.

(2) The classification of external roof surfaces is explained in Appendix A.

(3) No limit in the case of any space described in 2a, b and c.

(4) Single skin rooflight only, in the case of non-thermoplastic material.

(5) The rooflight should also meet the provisions of Diagram 42.

Polycarbonate and PVC rooflights which achieve a Class 1 rating by test, see paragraph 14.6, may be regarded as having an AA designation.

None of the above designations are suitable for protected stairways - see paragraph 6.10.

Products may have upper and lower surfaces with different properties if they have double skins or are laminates of different materials.

The Requirement

This Approved Document which takes effect on
1 June 1992, deals with the following
Requirement from Part B of Schedule 1 to the
Building Regulations 1991:

Requirement	Limits on application
Access and facilities for the fire service **B5.** (1) The building shall be designed and constructed so as to provide facilities to assist fire fighters in the protection of life. (2) Provision shall be made within the site of the building to enable fire appliances to gain access to the building.	

Guidance

Performance

In the Secretary of State's view the requirement of B5 will be met:

a. if there is sufficient means of external access to enable fire appliances to be brought near to the building for effective use;

b. if there is sufficient means of access into, and within, the building for fire-fighting personnel to effect rescue and fight fire; and

c. if the building is provided with sufficient internal fire mains and other facilities to assist fire fighters in their tasks;

d. if the building is provided with adequate means for venting heat and smoke from a fire in a basement.

These access arrangements and facilities are only required in the interests of the health and safety of people in and around the building. The extent to which they are required will depend on the use and size of the building in so far as it affects the health and safety of those people.

Introduction

*0.53 The guidance given here covers the selection and design of facilities for the purpose of protecting life by assisting the fire service.

To assist the fire service some or all of the following facilities may be necessary, depending mainly on the size of the building:

a.   vehicle access for fire appliances

b.   access for fire fighting personnel

c.   the provision of fire mains within the building

d.   venting for heat and smoke from basement areas.

Facilities appropriate to a specific building
0.54 The main factor determining the facilities needed to assist the fire service is the size of the building. Generally speaking fire fighting is carried out within the building.

a.   In deep basements and tall buildings (see paragraph 17.2) fire fighters will invariably work inside. They need special access facilities (see Section 17), equipped with fire mains, (see Section 15). Fire appliances will need access to entry points near the fire mains, (see Section 16).

b. In other buildings the combination of personnel access facilities offered by the normal means of escape, and the ability to work from ladders and appliances on the perimeter, will generally be adequate without special internal arrangements. Vehicle access may be needed to some or all of the perimeter, depending on the size of the building. (see Section 16).

c. Products of combustion from basement fires tend to escape via stairways, making access difficult for fire service personnel. The problem can be reduced by providing vents. Venting can improve visibility and reduce temperatures, making search, rescue and fire fighting less difficult.

* Introductory paragraphs 0.49 - 0.52 are on page 71.

Section 15

FIRE MAINS

Introduction

15.1 Fire mains are installed in a building and equipped (with valves etc.) so that the fire service may connect hoses for water to fight fires inside the building. Rising fire mains serve floors above ground, or upwards from the level at which the fire service gain access, (called the access level) if this is not ground level. (In a podium design for instance the access level may be above the ground level, see Diagram 45). Falling mains serve levels below ground or access level.

Fire mains may be of the 'dry' type which are normally empty and are supplied through hose from a fire service pumping appliance. Alternately they may be 'wet' type where they are kept full of water and supplied from tanks and pumps in the building. There should be a facility to allow a wet system to be replenished from a pumping appliance in an emergency.

Provision of fire mains

15.2 Buildings provided with firefighting shafts should be provided with fire mains in those shafts. The criteria for the provision of firefighting shafts are given in Section 17.

15.3 Wet rising mains should be provided in buildings with a floor at more than 60m above ground or access level. In lower buildings where fire mains are provided either wet or dry mains are suitable.

Number and location of fire mains

15.4 There should be one fire main in every firefighting shaft. (See Section 17 for guidance on the provision of firefighting shafts).

15.5 The outlets from fire mains should be sited in each firefighting lobby giving access to accommodation from a firefighting shaft. (See Section 17 paragraphs 17.9 and 17.10.)

Design and construction of fire mains

15.6 Guidance on other aspects of the design and construction of fire mains, not included in the provisions of this Approved Document, should be obtained from sections 2 and 3 of BS 5306: Part 1.

Section 16

VEHICLE ACCESS

Introduction

16.1 For the purposes of this Approved Document vehicle access to the exterior of a building is needed to enable high reach appliances, such as turntable ladders and hydraulic platforms, to be used, and to enable pumping appliances to supply water and equipment for firefighting and rescue activities.

Access requirements increase with building size and height.

Fire mains (see Section 15) enable fire fighters within the building to connect their hoses to a water supply. In buildings fitted with fire mains, pumping appliances need access to the perimeter at points near the mains, where firefighters can enter the building and where in the case of dry mains, a hose connection will be made from the appliance to pump water into the main.

The vehicle access requirements described in Table 19 for buildings without fire mains, do not apply to buildings with fire mains.

Vehicle access routes and hardstandings should meet the criteria described in Diagram 44 and paragraphs 16.8 to 16.10 if they are to be used by fire service vehicles.

Buildings not fitted with fire mains
16.2 There should be vehicle access to small buildings (those of up to 2000m^2 with a top storey less than 9m above ground level) to within 45m of any point on the projected plan area (or 'footprint' (see Diagram 43)) of the building or to 15% of the perimeter whichever is the less onerous. (However, it should be noted that requirements cannot be made under the Building Regulations for work to be done outside the site of the works shown on the deposited plans, building notice or initial notice.)

16.3 Vehicle access to buildings that do not have fire mains should be provided in accordance with Table 19.

16.4 Any elevation to which vehicle access is provided in accordance with Table 19 should have a suitable door, not less than 750mm wide, giving access to the interior of the building.

Buildings fitted with fire mains
16.5 Fire mains should be provided in buildings which have firefighting shafts (see Section 17).

Table 19 Fire service vehicle access to buildings not fitted with fire mains

Total floor[1] area of building m^2	Height of floor of top storey above ground[2]	Provide vehicle access to:	Type of appliance
up to 2000	up to 9	see paragraph 16.2	pump
	over 9	15% of perimeter[3]	high reach
2000-8000	up to 9	15% of perimeter	pump
	over 9	50% of perimeter[3]	high reach
8000-16,000	up to 9	50% of perimeter[3]	pump
	over 9	50% of perimeter[3]	high reach
16,000-24,000	up to 9	75% of perimeter[3]	pump
	over 9	75% of perimeter[3]	high reach
over 24,000	up to 9	100% of perimeter[3]	pump
	over 9	100% of perimeter[3]	high reach

Notes
Provisions about the design of vehicle access routes are given in paragraphs 16.8 to 16.10 and Diagram 44.
1. The total floor area is the aggregate of all the floors in the building.
2. In the case of purpose group 7(a) (storage) buildings, height should be measured to mean roof level, see methods of measurement in Appendix C.
3. Perimeter is described in Diagram 43.

Diagram 43 Example of building footprint and perimeter

See para 16.2

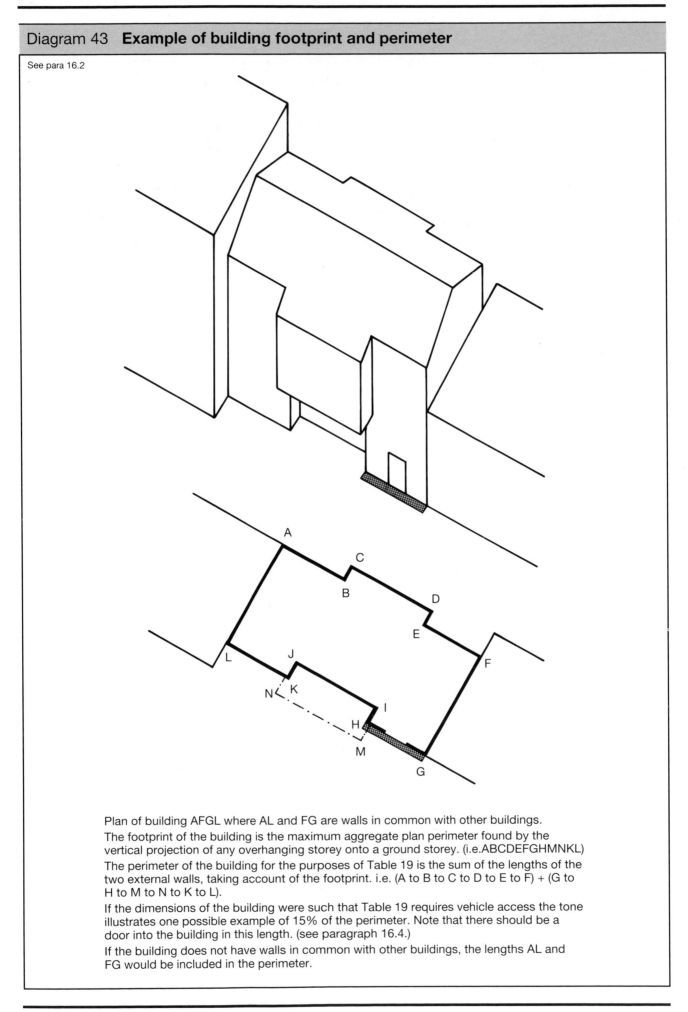

Plan of building AFGL where AL and FG are walls in common with other buildings.

The footprint of the building is the maximum aggregate plan perimeter found by the vertical projection of any overhanging storey onto a ground storey. (i.e.ABCDEFGHMNKL)

The perimeter of the building for the purposes of Table 19 is the sum of the lengths of the two external walls, taking account of the footprint. i.e. (A to B to C to D to E to F) + (G to H to M to N to K to L).

If the dimensions of the building were such that Table 19 requires vehicle access the tone illustrates one possible example of 15% of the perimeter. Note that there should be a door into the building in this length. (see paragraph 16.4.)

If the building does not have walls in common with other buildings, the lengths AL and FG would be included in the perimeter.

Table 20 Typical vehicle access route specification

Appliance Type	Minimum width of road between kerbs (m)	minimum width of gateways (m)	minimum turning circle between kerbs (m)	minimum turning circle between walls (m)	minimum clearance height (m)	minimum carrying capacity (tonnes)
Pump	3.7	3.1	16.8	19.2	3.7	12.5
High Reach	3.7	3.1	26.0	29.0	4.0	17.0

Notes

1. Fire appliances are not standardised. Some fire services have appliances of greater weight or different size. In consultation with the Fire Authority, Building Control Authorities and Approved Inspectors may adopt other dimensions in such circumstances.

2. Because the weight of high reach appliances is distributed over a number of axles, it is considered that their infrequent use of a carriageway or route designed to 12.5 tonnes should not cause damage. It would therefore be reasonable to design the roadbase to 12.5 tonnes, although structures such as bridges should have the full 17 tonnes capacity.

16.6 In the case of a building fitted with dry fire mains there should be access for a pumping appliance to within 18m of each fire main inlet connection point. The inlet should be visible from the appliance.

16.7 In the case of a building fitted with wet mains the pumping appliance access should be to within 18m, and within sight of, a suitable entrance giving access to the main, and in sight of the inlet for the emergency replenishment of the suction tank for the main.

Design of access routes and hardstandings
16.8 A vehicle access route may be a road, or other route, which, including any manhole covers and the like, meets the standards in Table 20, Diagram 44 and the following paragraphs.

16.9 Where access is provided to an elevation in accordance with Table 20, overhead obstructions such as cables and branches that would interfere with the setting of ladders etc, should be avoided in the zone shown in Diagram 44.

16.10 Turning facilities should be provided in any dead-end access route that is more than 20m long. This can be by a hammerhead or turning circle, designed on the basis of Table 20.

Diagram 44 Relationship between building and hardstanding/access roads for high reach fire appliances

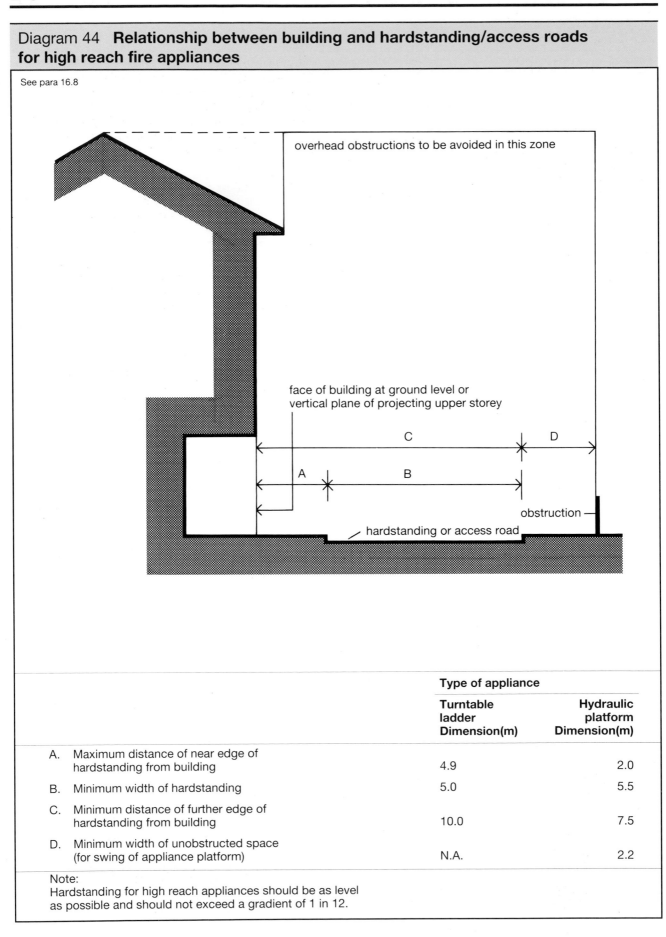

See para 16.8

overhead obstructions to be avoided in this zone

face of building at ground level or
vertical plane of projecting upper storey

C   D

A   B

obstruction

hardstanding or access road

		Type of appliance	
		Turntable ladder Dimension(m)	Hydraulic platform Dimension(m)
A.	Maximum distance of near edge of hardstanding from building	4.9	2.0
B.	Minimum width of hardstanding	5.0	5.5
C.	Minimum distance of further edge of hardstanding from building	10.0	7.5
D.	Minimum width of unobstructed space (for swing of appliance platform)	N.A.	2.2

Note:
Hardstanding for high reach appliances should be as level
as possible and should not exceed a gradient of 1 in 12.

Section 17

ACCESS TO BUILDINGS FOR FIRE-FIGHTING PERSONNEL

Introduction

17.1 In low rise buildings without deep basements fire service personnel access requirements will be met by a combination of the normal means of escape, and the measures for vehicle access in Section 16, which facilitate ladder access to upper storeys. In other buildings the problems of reaching the fire, and working inside near the fire, necessitate the provision of additional facilities to avoid delay and to provide a sufficiently secure operating base to allow effective action to be taken.

These additional facilities include firefighting lifts, firefighting stairs and firefighting lobbies, which are combined in a protected shaft known as the firefighting shaft (Diagram 46).

Guidance on protected shafts in general is given in Section 8.

Provision of firefighting shafts

17.2 Buildings with a floor at more than 20m above ground or fire service access level, or with a basement at more than 10m below ground or access level, should be provided with firefighting shafts containing firefighting lifts. (See Diagram 45.)

17.3 Buildings other than open sided car parks (see 11.4) with a storey of 600m² or more in area, where the floor is at a height of more than 7.5m above ground or access level, should be provided with firefighting shaft(s), which need not include firefighting lifts.

17.4 Buildings with two or more basement storeys, each exceeding 900m² in area, should be provided with firefighting shaft(s), which need not include firefighting lifts.

17.5 If a firefighting shaft is required to serve a basement it need not also serve the upper floors unless they also qualify because of the height or size of the building. Similarly a shaft serving upper storeys need not serve a basement which is not large or deep enough to qualify in its own right. However, a firefighting stair and any firefighting lift should serve all intermediate storeys between the highest and lowest storeys that they serve.

Diagram 45 Provision of fire-fighting shafts

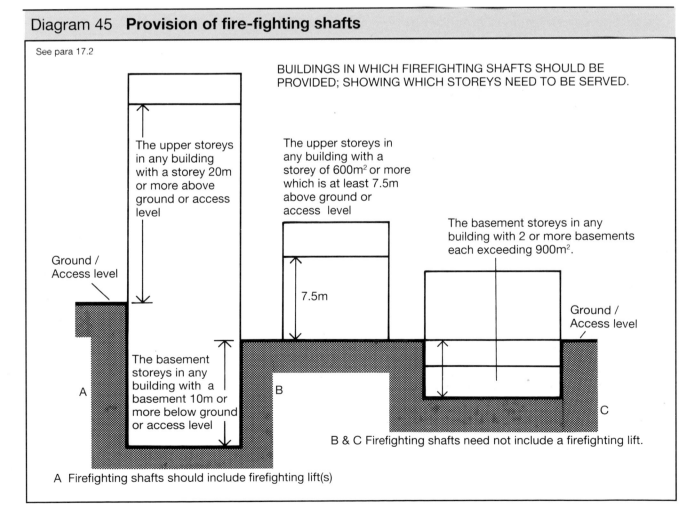

See para 17.2

BUILDINGS IN WHICH FIREFIGHTING SHAFTS SHOULD BE PROVIDED; SHOWING WHICH STOREYS NEED TO BE SERVED.

The upper storeys in any building with a storey 20m or more above ground or access level

The upper storeys in any building with a storey of 600m² or more which is at least 7.5m above ground or access level

The basement storeys in any building with 2 or more basements each exceeding 900m².

Ground / Access level

7.5m

Ground / Access level

The basement storeys in any building with a basement 10m or more below ground or access level

A

B

C

B & C Firefighting shafts need not include a firefighting lift.

A Firefighting shafts should include firefighting lift(s)

17.6 Shopping complexes should be provided with firefighting shafts in accordance with the recommendations of Section 3 of BS 5588: Part 10.

Number and location of firefighting shafts

17.7 The number of firefighting shafts should:

a. comply with Table 21, if the building is fitted throughout with an automatic sprinkler system meeting the relevant recommendations of BS 5306: Part 2; or

b. if the building is not fitted with sprinklers be such that there is at least one for every 900m² (or part thereof) of floor area of the largest floor that is more than 20m above ground level (or above 7.5m in the case of paragraph 17.3).

c. the same 900m² per firefighting shaft criterion should be applied to calculate the number of shafts needed where basements require them.

17.8 The location of firefighting shafts should be such that every part of every storey, other than fire service access level, is no more than 60m from the entrance to a firefighting lobby, measured on a route suitable for laying hose. If the internal layout is unknown at the design stage, then every part of every such storey should be no more than 40m in a direct line from the entrance to a firefighting lobby.

Design and construction of firefighting shafts

17.9 Every firefighting stairway and firefighting lift should be approached, from the accommodation, through a firefighting lobby.

17.10 All firefighting shafts should be equipped with fire mains having outlet connections and valves in every firefighting lobby except at access level.

17.11 Firefighting shafts should be designed, constructed and installed in accordance with the recommendations of BS 5588: Part 5 in respect of the following:

a. Section 2: Planning and construction

b. Section 3: Firefighting lift installation

c. Section 4: Electrical services

Diagram 46 Components of a firefighting shaft

See para 17.1

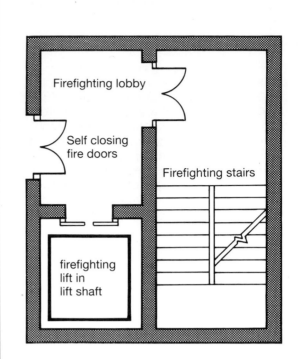

Notes

1. Outlets from a fire main should be located in the firefighting lobby except at access level.

2. A firefighting lift is required if the building has a floor 20m or more above, or 10m or more below ground or access level.

3. This Diagram is only to illustrate the basic components and is not meant to represent the only acceptable layout. Ventilation measures have not been shown (refer to BS 5588: Part 5).

Table 21 Minimum number of firefighting shafts in building fitted with sprinklers

Largest qualifying floor area (m²)	Minimum number of firefighting shafts
less than 900	1
900-2000	2
over 2000	2 plus 1 for every additional 1500m² or part thereof

Section 18

VENTING OF HEAT AND SMOKE FROM BASEMENTS

Introduction

18.1 In addition to any measures that may be needed to keep smoke from prejudicing the use of any firefighting shafts, there can be a need to remove smoke and heat from basements. Products of combustion from basement fires tend to escape via stairways, making access difficult for fire service personnel. The problem can be reduced by providing outlets for the heat and smoke. Venting can improve visibility and reduce temperatures, making search, rescue and fire fighting less difficult.

18.2 Smoke outlets (also referred to as smoke vents) provide a route for heat and smoke to escape to the open air from the basement level(s). They can also be used by the fire service to let cooler air into the basement(s). (See Diagram 47).

Provision of smoke outlets

18.3 Where practicable each basement space should have one or more smoke outlets, but it is not always possible to do this where, for example, the plan is deep and the amount of external wall is restricted by adjoining buildings. It is therefore acceptable to vent spaces on the perimeter and allow other spaces to be vented indirectly by firefighters opening connecting doors. However if a basement is compartmented, each compartment should have direct access to venting, without having to open doors etc. into another compartment.

18.4 Smoke outlets, connected directly to the open air, should be provided from every basement storey, except for:

a. a basement in a single family dwellinghouse of purpose group 1(b) or 1(c); or

b. any basement storey that has:

i. a floor area of not more than 200m^2; and

ii. a floor not more than 3m below the adjacent ground level.

18.5 Strong rooms need not be provided with smoke outlets.

Natural smoke outlets

18.6 Smoke outlets should be sited at high level, either in the ceiling or in the wall of the space they serve. They should be evenly distributed around the perimeter of the building, to discharge in the open air outside the building.

Diagram 47 Fire resisting construction for smoke outlet shafts

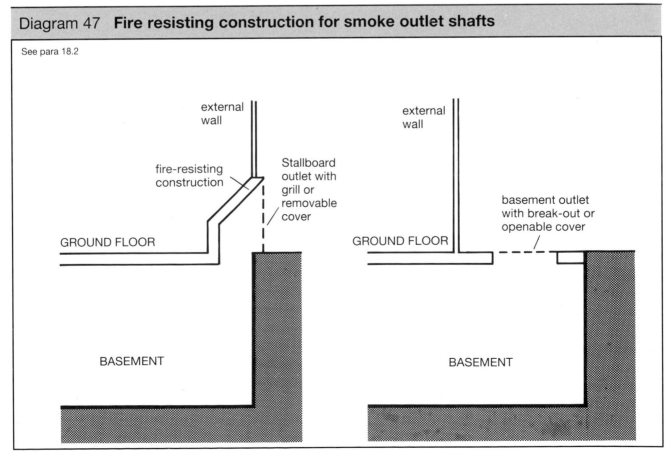

See para 18.2

external wall

fire-resisting construction

Stallboard outlet with grill or removable cover

GROUND FLOOR

BASEMENT

external wall

basement outlet with break-out or openable cover

GROUND FLOOR

BASEMENT

Approved Document

Access and facilities for the fire service

18.7 The combined clear cross-sectional area of all smoke outlets should not be less than 2.5% of the floor area of the storey they serve.

18.8 Separate outlets should be provided from places of special fire risk.

18.9 If the outlet terminates at a point that is not readily accessible it should be kept unobstructed, and should only be covered with a non combustible grille or louvre.

18.10 If the outlet terminates in a readily accessible position it may be covered by a panel, stallboard or pavement light which can be broken out or opened. The position of such covered outlets should be suitably indicated.

18.11 Outlets should not be placed where they would prevent the use of escape routes from the building.

Mechanical smoke extract

18.12 A system of mechanical extraction may be provided as an alternative to natural venting, to remove smoke and heat from basements, provided that the basement storey(s) are fitted with a sprinkler system. The sprinkler system should be in accordance with the principles of BS 5306: Part 2. (It is not considered necessary in this particular case to install sprinklers on the storeys other than the basement(s) unless they are needed for other reasons).

18.13 The air extraction system should give at least 10 air changes per hour, and should be capable of handling gas temperatures of 400°C for not less than one hour. It should come into operation automatically on activation of the sprinkler system, alternatively activation may be by an automatic fire detection system which conforms to BS 5839: Part 1 (at least L3 standard).

Construction of outlet ducts or shafts

18.14 Outlet ducts or shafts, including any bulkheads over them (see Diagram 47) should be enclosed by non-combustible fire resisting construction.

18.15 Where there are natural smoke outlet shafts from different compartments of the same basement storey, or from different basement storeys, they should be separated from each other by non-combustible fire resisting construction.

Basement car parks

18.16 The provisions for ventilation of basement car parks in Section 11 may be taken as satisfying the requirements in respect of the need for smoke venting from any basement that is used as a car park.

Appendix A

PERFORMANCE OF MATERIALS AND STRUCTURES

General

A1 Much of the guidance in this document is given in terms of performance in relation to British Standard methods of test identified below. In such cases the material, product or structure should:

a.   be shown by test to be capable of meeting that performance, or

b.   have been assessed against appropriate standards as meeting that performance. (For this purpose suitably qualified fire safety engineers, laboratories accredited by NAMAS for conducting the relevant test, the BRE, and other bodies such as the BBA, might be expected to have the necessary expertise), or

c.   where tables of notional performance are included in this document, conform with an appropriate specification given in these tables, or

d.   (in the case of fire-resisting elements) conform with an appropriate specification given in Part II of the Building Research Establishments' Report *'Guidelines for the construction of fire resisting structural elements'* (BRE, 1988).

Note: Guidance on increasing the fire resistance of existing timber floors is given in BRE Digest 208 (BRE 1988).

A2 Building Regulations deal with fire safety in buildings as a whole. Thus they are aimed at limiting fire hazard.

The aim of standard fire tests is to measure or assess the response of a material, product, structure or system to one or more aspects of fire behaviour. Standard fire tests cannot normally measure fire hazard. They form only one of a number of factors that need to be taken into account. Other factors are those set out in these documents.

Fire resistance

A3 Factors having a bearing on fire resistance, that are considered in this document, are:

a.   fire severity,

b.   building height, and

c.   building occupancy,

A4 The standards of fire resistance given are based on assumptions about the severity of fires and the consequences should an element fail. Fire severity is estimated in very broad terms from the use of the building (its purpose group), on the assumption that the building contents (which constitute the fire load) are the same for buildings in the same use.

A number of factors affect the standard of fire resistance specified. These are:

a.   the amount of combustible material per unit of floor area in various types of building (the fire load density);

b.   the height of the top floor above ground, which affects the ease of escape and of fire fighting operations, and the consequences should large scale collapse occur;

c.   occupancy, which reflects the ease with which the building can be evacuated quickly;

d.   whether there are basements, because the lack of an external wall through which to vent heat and smoke may increase heat build-up, and thus affect the duration of a fire, as well as complicating fire-fighting; and

e.   whether the building is of single storey construction (where escape is direct and structural failure is unlikely to precede evacuation).

Because the use of buildings may change, a precise estimate of fire severity based on the fire load due to a particular use may be misleading. Therefore if a fire engineering approach of this kind is adopted the likelihood that the fire load may change in the future needs to be considered.

A5 Performance in terms of the fire resistance to be met by elements of structure, doors and other forms of construction is determined by reference to BS 476: Parts 20-24: 1987 (or to BS 476: Part 8: 1972 in respect of items tested or assessed prior to 1 January 1988) in respect of one or more of the following criteria:

a.   resistance to collapse (loadbearing capacity), which applies to loadbearing elements;

b.   resistance to fire penetration (integrity), which applies to fire separating elements; and

c.   resistance to the transfer of excessive heat (insulation), which applies to fire separating elements.

Table A1 gives the specific requirements for each element in terms of the three performance criteria above. (Provisions for fire doors are set out in Appendix B, Table B1.)

Table A2 sets out the minimum periods of fire resistance for elements of structure.

Table A3 sets out criteria appropriate to the suspended ceilings that can be accepted as contributing to the fire resistance of a floor.

Table A4 sets out limitations on the use of uninsulated fire-resisting glazed elements. These limitations do not apply to the use of insulated fire-resisting glazed elements.

Information on tests on fire-resisting elements is given in the following publications:

Fire Protection Association
Fire test results on building products: fire resistance, 1983. (Available from the FPA, 140 Aldersgate Street, London ECIA 4HX).

Association of Structural Fire Protection Contractors and Manufacturers
Fire protection for structural steel in buildings, second edition,1988. (Available from the ASFPCM, PO Box 111, Aldershot, Hants, GU11 1YW).

Loss Prevention Council
Rules for the construction and installation of firebreak doors and shutters, 1988. (Available from the FPA, 140 Aldersgate Street, London ECIA 4HX).

Information on tested elements is also frequently given in literature available from manufacturers and trade associations.

Any reference used to substantiate the fire resistance rating of a construction should be carefully checked to ensure that it is suitable, adequate and applicable to the construction to be used. Small differences in detail (such as fixing method, joints, dimensions, etc) may significantly affect the rating.

Roofs
A6 Performance in terms of the resistance of roofs to external fire exposure is determined by reference to the methods specified in BS 476: Part 3: 1958 under which constructions are designated by 2 letters in the range A to D, with an AA designation being the best. The first letter indicates the time to penetration, and the second letter a measure of the spread of flame. Note that this is not the most recent version of the standard.

In some circumstances roofs, or parts of roofs, may need to be fire resisting, for example if used as an escape route or if the roof performs the function of a floor. Such circumstances are covered in Sections 3 and 7.

Table A5 gives notional designations of some generic roof coverings.

Non-combustible materials
A7 Non-combustible materials are defined in Table A6 either as listed products, or in terms of performance when tested to BS 476: Part 4: 1970 or Part 11: 1982.

Only these materials may be used where there is a provision for non-combustibility and also for the specific applications in the elements listed in Table A6. Non-combustible materials may be used whenever there is a requirement for materials of limited combustibility.

Materials of limited combustibility
A8 Materials of limited combustibility are defined in Table A7 by reference to the method specified in BS 476: Part 11: 1982. Table A7 also includes composite products (such as plasterboard) which are considered acceptable, and where these are exposed as linings they should also meet any appropriate flame spread rating.

Internal linings
A9 Flame spread over wall or ceiling surfaces is controlled by providing for the lining materials or products to meet given performance levels in tests appropriate to the materials or products involved.

A10 To restrict the use of materials which ignite easily, which have a high rate of heat release and/or which reduce the time to flashover, maximum acceptable 'fire propagation' indices are specified. These are determined by reference to the method specified in BS 476: Part 6: 1981 or 1989. Index of performance (I) relates to the overall test performance, whereas sub-index (i_1) is derived from the first three minutes of test.

A11 Lining systems which can be effectively tested for 'surface spread of flame' are rated for performance by reference to the method specified in BS 476: Part 7: 1971 or 1987 under which materials or products are classified 1, 2, 3 or 4 with Class 1 being the highest.

A12 The highest product performance classification for lining materials is Class 0. This is achieved if a material or the surface of a composite product is either:

a. composed throughout of materials of limited combustibility, or

b. a Class 1 material which has a fire propagation index (I) of not more than 12 and subindex (i_1) of not more than 6.

Note: Class 0 is not a classification identified in any British Standard test.

A13 Composite products defined as materials of limited combustibility (see A8 and Table A7) should in addition comply with the test requirement appropriate to any surface rating specified in the guidance on requirements B2, B3 and B4.

A14 The notional performance ratings of certain widely used generic materials or products are listed in Table A8 in terms of their performance in the traditional lining tests BS 476: Parts 6 and 7.

A15 Results of tests on proprietary materials are frequently given in literature available from manufacturers and trade associations.

Any reference used to substantiate the surface spread of flame rating of a material or product should be carefully checked to ensure that it is suitable, adequate and applicable to the construction to be used. Small differences in detail, such as thickness, substrate, colour, form, fixings, adhesive etc, may significantly affect the rating.

Thermoplastic materials

A16 A thermoplastic material means any synthetic polymeric material which has a softening point below 200°C if tested to BS 2782: Part 1: Method 120A: 1976. Specimens for this test may be fabricated from the original polymer where the thickness of material of the end product is less than 2.5mm.

A17 A thermoplastic material in isolation can not be assumed to protect a substrate, when used as a lining to a wall or ceiling. The surface rating of both products must therefore meet the required classification. If however, the thermoplastic material is fully bonded to a non-thermoplastic substrate, then only the surface rating of the composite will need to comply.

A18 Concessions are made for thermoplastic materials used for windows, rooflights, and lighting diffusers within suspended ceilings, which may not comply with the criteria specified in paragraphs A10 et seq. They are described in the guidance on requirements B2 and B4.

A19 For the purposes of the requirements B2 and B4 thermoplastic materials should either be used according to their classification 0-3, under the BS 476: parts 6 and 7 tests as described in paragraphs A10 et seq., if they have such a rating, or they may be classified TP(a) rigid, TP(a) flexible, or TP(b) according to the following methods:

TP(a) rigid:
i.   Rigid solid pvc sheet;

ii. solid (as distinct from double- or multiple-skin) polycarbonate sheet at least 3mm thick;

iii. multi-skinned rigid sheet made from unplasticised pvc or polycarbonate which has Class 1 rating when tested to BS 476: Part 7 1971 or 1987

iv. any other rigid thermoplastic product, a specimen of which, when tested to BS 2782: 1970 as amended in 1974: method 508A, performs so that the test flame extinguishes before the first mark, and the duration of flaming or afterglow does not exceed 5 seconds following removal of the burner.

TP(a) flexible:
Flexible products not more than 1mm thick which comply with the Type C requirements of BS 5867: Part 2 when tested to BS 5438, Test 2 1989 with the flame applied to the surface of the specimens for 5, 15, 20 and 30 seconds respectively, but excluding the cleansing procedure; and

TP(b):
i.   Rigid solid polycarbonate sheet products less than 3mm thick, or multiple skin polycarbonate sheet products which do not qualify as TP(a) by test; or

ii. Other products which, when a specimen of the material between 1.5 and 3mm thick is tested in accordance with BS 2782: 1970, as amended in 1974: method 508A, has a rate of burning which does not exceed 50mm/minute. (If it is not possible to cut or machine a 3mm thick specimen from the product then a 3mm test specimen can be moulded from the same material as that used for the manufacture of the product).

Fire test methods

A20 A guide to the various test methods in BS 476 and BS 2782 is given in PD 6520: 1988 (available from the British Standards Institution).

A guide to the development and presentation of fire tests and their use in hazard assessment is given in BS 6336: 1982.

Table A1   Specific provisions of test for fire resistance of elements of structure etc.

Part of building	Minimum provisions when tested to the relevant part of BS 476(1) (minutes)			Method of exposure
	Loadbearing capacity(2)	Integrity	Insulation	
1. Structural frame, beam or column	see Table A2	not applicable	not applicable	exposed faces
2. Loadbearing wall (which is not also a wall described in any of the following items)	see Table A2	not applicable	not applicable	each side separately
3. Floors: a. in upper storey of 2 storey dwellinghouse (but not over garage)	30	15	15	from underside(3)
b. any other floor including compartment floors	see Table A2	see Table A2	see Table A2	
4. Roofs: a. any part forming an escape route	30	30	30	from underside(3)
b. any roof that performs the function of a floor	see Table A2	see Table A2	see Table A2	
5. External walls: a. any part less than 1m from any point on the relevant boundary	see Table A2	see Table A2	see Table A2	each side separately
b. any part 1m or more from the relevant boundary	see Table A2	see Table A2	15(4)	from inside
6. Compartment walls separating occupancies (see 8.10)	60 or see Table A2 (whichever is less)	60 or see Table A2 (whichever is less)	60 or see Table A2 (whichever is less)	each side separately
7. Compartment wall other than 6.	see Table A2	see Table A2	see Table A2	each side separately
8. Protected shafts, excluding any firefighting shaft: a. any glazing described in Approved Document B3 Diagram 26	not applicable	30	no provision(5)	each
b. any other part between the shaft and a protected lobby/corridor described in Diagram 26 above	30	30	30	side
c. any part not described in (a) or (b) above	see Table A2	see Table A2	see Table A2	separately
9. Enclosure (which does not form part of a compartment wall or a protected shaft) to a:				
a. protected stairway	30	30	30(6)	each
b. lift shaft	30	30	30	side
c. service shaft	30	30	30	separately
10. Firefighting shafts: a. construction separating fire-fighting shaft from rest of building	120	120	120	from side remote from shaft
	60	60	60	from shaft side
b. construction separating fire-fighting stairway, firefighting lift shaft and firefighting lobby	60	60	60	each side separately

Table A1 **continued**

Part of building	Minimum provisions when tested to the relevant part of BS 476(1) (minutes)			Method of exposure
	Loadbearing capacity(2)	Integrity	Insulation	
11. Enclosure (which is not a compartment wall or described in item 8) to a:				
a. protected lobby	30	30	30(6)	each side separately
b. protected corridor	30	30	30(6)	
12. Subdivision of a corridor	30	30	30(6)	each side separately
13. Wall separating an attached or integral garage from a dwellinghouse	30	30	30(6)	from garage side
14. Enclosure in a flat or maisonette to a protected entrance hall, or to a protected landing	30	30	30(6)	each side separately
15. Fire-resisting construction a. enclosing communal areas in sheltered housing	30	30	30	each side separately
b. in dwellings not described elsewhere	30	30	30(6)	
16. Cavity barrier	not applicable	30	15	each side separately
17. Ceiling described in Section 9 Diagram 29 or Diagram 31	not applicable	30	30	from underside
18. Duct described in paragraph 9.14(e)	not applicable	30	no provision	from outside
19. Casing around a drainage system described in Section 10 Diagram 34	not applicable	30	no provision	from outside
20. Flue walls described in Section 10 Diagram 35	not applicable	see Table A2	see Table A2	from outside
21. Fire doors		see Table B1		

Notes:

1. Part 21 for loadbearing elements, Part 22 for non-loadbearing elements, Part 23 for fire-protecting suspended ceilings, and Part 24 for ventilation ducts. BS 476: Part 8 results are acceptable for items tested or assessed before 1st January 1988.

2. Applies to loadbearing elements only.

3. A suspended ceiling should only be relied on to contribute to the fire resistance of the floor if the ceiling meets the appropriate provisions given in Table A3.

4. 30 minutes for any part adjacent to an external escape route (but no provision for glazed elements in respect of insulation).

5. Except for any limitations on glazed elements given in Table A4.

6. See Table A4 for permitted extent of uninsulated glazed elements.

Table A2 Minimum periods of fire resistance

Purpose group of building	Minimum periods (minutes) for elements of structure in a:					
	Basement storey($) including floor over		Ground or upper storey			
	Depth(m) of a lowest basement		Height(m) of top floor above ground, in building or separated part of building			
	more than 10	not more than 10	not more than 5	not more than 20	not more than 30	more than 30
1. Residential (domestic): a. flats and maisonettes	90	60	30*	60**†	90**	120**
b. and c. dwellinghouses	not relevant	30*	30*	60@	not relevant	not relevant
2. Residential: a. Institutional~ b. other residential	90 90	60 60	30* 30*	60 60	90 90	120# 120#
3. Office: - not sprinklered - sprinklered(2)	90 60	60 60	30* 30*	60 30*	90 60	not permitted 120#
4. Shop and commercial: - not sprinklered - sprinklered(2)	90 60	60 60	60 30*	60 60	90 60	not permitted 120#
5. Assembly and recreation: - not sprinklered - sprinklered(2)	90 60	60 60	60 30*	60 60	90 60	not permitted 120#
6. Industrial: - not sprinklered - sprinklered(2)	120 90	90 60	60 30*	90 60	120 90	not permitted 120#
7. Storage & other non-residential: a. any building or part not described elsewhere: - not sprinklered - sprinklered(2)	120 90	90 60	60 30*	90 60	120 90	not permitted 120#
b. car park for light vehicles: i. open sided park(3) ii. any other park	not applicable 90	not applicable 60	15*+ 30*	15*+ 60	15*+ 90	60 120#

Modifications referred to in Table A2: [for notes and application of the table see next page]

$ The floor over a basement (or if there is more than 1 basement, the floor over the topmost basement) should meet the provisions for the ground and upper storeys if that period is higher.

*   Increased to a minimum of 60 minutes for compartment walls separating buildings

**   Reduced to 30 minutes for any floor within a maisonette, but not if the floor contributes to the support of the building

~   Multi-storey hospitals designed in accordance with the NHS Firecode documents should have a minimum 60 minutes standard

Reduced to 90 minutes for elements not forming part of the structural frame

+   Increased to 30 minutes for elements protecting the means of escape

†   Refer to 7.12 regarding the acceptability of 30 minutes in flat conversions

@   30 minutes in the case of three storey dwelling houses increased to 60 minutes minimum for compartment walls separating buildings.

Notes to Table A2:

1. Refer to Table A1 for the specific provisions of test.

2. "Sprinklered" means that the building is fitted throughout with an automatic sprinkler system meeting the relevant recommendations of BS 5306: Part 2; ie. the relevant occupancy rating together with the additional requirements for life safety.

3. The car park should comply with the relevant provisions in the guidance on requirement B3, section 11.

Application of the fire resistance standards in Table A2:

a. Where one element of structure supports or carries or gives stability to another, the fire resistance of the supporting element should be no less than the minimum period of fire resistance for the other element (whether that other element is loadbearing or not).

There are circumstances where it may be reasonable to vary this principle, for example:

i. where the supporting structure is in the open air, and is not likely to be affected by the fire in the building; or

ii. the supporting structure is in a different compartment, with a fire separating element (which has the higher standard of fire resistance) between the supporting and the supported structure.

b. Where an element of structure forms part of more than one building or compartment, that element should be constructed to the standard of the greater of the relevant provisions.

c. Where one side of a basement is (due to the slope of the ground) open at ground level, giving an opportunity for smoke venting and access for fire fighting, it may be appropriate to adopt the standard of fire resistance applicable to above-ground structures for elements of structure in that storey.

d. Although some elements of structure in a single storey building may be excluded from needing fire resistance (see the guidance on requirement B3, paragraph 7.4(a)), fire resistance will be needed if the element:

i. is part of (or supports) an external wall and there is provision in the guidance on requirement B4 to limit the extent of openings and other unprotected areas in the wall; or

ii. is part of (or supports) a compartment wall, including a wall common to two or more buildings, or a wall between a dwelling house and an attached or integral garage; or

iii. supports a gallery.

For the purposes of this paragraph, the ground storey of a building which has one or more basement storeys and no upper storeys, may be considered as single storey building. The fire resistance of the basement storeys should be that appropriate to basements.

e. Single storey buildings are subject to the periods under the heading "not more than 5". If they have basements the basement storeys are subject to the period appropriate to their depth.

Table A3 Limitations on fire-protecting suspended ceilings

Height of building or separated part (m)	Type of floor	Provision for fire resistance of floor (minutes)	description of suspended ceiling
less than 20	not compartment	60 or less	Type A,B,C or D
	compartment	less than 60	
		60	Type B,C, or D
20 or more	any	60 or less	Type C or D
no limit	any	more than 60	Type D

Notes to Table A3

Ceiling type and description

A. Surface of ceiling exposed to the cavity should be Class 0 or Class 1.

B. Surface of ceiling exposed to the cavity should be Class 0.

C. Surface of ceiling exposed to the cavity should be Class 0. Ceiling should not contain easily openable access panels.

D. Ceiling should be of a material of limited combustibility and not contain easily openable access panels. Any insulation above the ceiling should be of a material of limited combustibility.

Any access panels provided in fire protecting suspended ceilings of type C or D should be secured in position by releasing devices or screw fixings, and they should be shown to have been tested in the ceiling assembly in which they are incorporated.

Table A4 **Limitations on the use of uninsulated glazed elements on escape routes.** (These limitations do not apply to glazed elements which satisfy the relevant insulation criterion, see Table A1)				
Position of glazed element	**Maximum total glazed area in parts of a building with access to:**			
	a single stairway		**more than one stairway**	
	walls	**door leaf**	**walls**	**door leaf**
1. Single family dwellinghouses within the enclosures of a protected stairway or within fire-resisting separation shown in Section 1 Diagram 2	fixed fanlights only	unlimited	fixed fanlights only	unlimited
2. Within the enclosures of a protected entrance hall or protected landing of a flat or maisonette	fixed fanlights only	unlimited above 1.1m from floor	fixed fanlights only	unlimited above 1.1m from floor
3. Between residential/sleeping accommodation and a common escape route (corridor, lobby or stair)	nil	nil	nil	nil
4. Between a protected stairway(1) and: i. the accommodation; or ii. a corridor which is not a protected corridor. Other than in item 3 above	nil	25% of door area	unlimited above 1.1m(2)	50% of door area
5. Between: i. a protected stairway and a protected lobby or protected corridor; or ii. accommodation and a protected lobby. Other than in item 3 above	unlimited above 1.1m from floor	unlimited above 0.1m from floor	unlimited above 0.1m from floor	unlimited above 0.1m from floor
6. Between the accommodation and a protected corridor forming a dead end. Other than in item 3 above.	unlimited above 1.1m from floor	unlimited above 0.1m from floor	unlimited above 0.1m from floor	unlimited above 0.1m from floor
7. Between accommodation and any other corridor; or subdividing corridors. Other than in item 3 above.	not applicable	not applicable	unlimited above 0.1m from floor	unlimited above 0.1m from floor

Notes

1. If the protected stairway is also a protected shaft (see paragraph 8.30) or a firefighting stair (see Section 17) there may be further restrictions on the uses of glazed elements.

2. Measured vertically from the landing floor level or the stair pitch line

Table A5 **Notional designations of roof coverings**

Part i: Pitched roofs covered with slates or tiles

Covering material	Supporting structure	Designation
1 Natural slates 2 Fibre reinforced cement slates 3 Clay tiles 4 Concrete tiles	1. timber rafters with or without underfelt, sarking, boarding, woodwool slabs, compressed straw slabs, plywood, wood chipboard, or fibre insulating board	AA
5 Bitumen felt strip slates Type 2E, with Type 2B underlayer bitumen felt	3. timber rafters and boarding, plywood, woodwool slabs, wood chipboard, or fibre insulating board	BB
6 Strip slates of bitumen felt, class 1 or 2	2. timber rafters and boarding, plywood, woodwool slabs, compressed straw slabs, wood chipboard, or fibre insulating board	CC

Note
Any reference in this table to bitumen felt of a specified type is a reference to bitumen felt as so designated in BS 747: 1977.

Part ii: Pitched roofs covered with self-supporting sheet

Roof covering material	Construction	Supporting structure	Designation
1. Profiled sheet of galvanised steel, aluminium, fibre reinforced cement, or pre-painted (coil coated) steel or aluminium with a pvc or pvf2 coating	1. Single skin without underlay, or with underlay of plasterboard, fibre insulating board, woodwool slab	Structure of timber, steel or concrete	AA
2. profiled sheet of galvanised steel, aluminium, fibre reinforced cement, or pre-painted (coil coated) steel or aluminium with a pvc or pvf2 coating	2. Double skin without interlayer, or with interlayer of resin bonded glass fibre, mineral wool slab, polystyrene, or polyurethane.	Structure of timber, steel or concrete	AA

Part iii: Flat roofs covered with bitumen felt

A flat roof comprising bitumen felt should (irrespective of the felt specification) be deemed to be of designation AA if the felt is laid on a deck constructed of any of the materials prescribed in the Table in part iv, and has a surface finish of:

a. bitumen-bedded stone chippings covering the whole surface to a depth of at least 12.5mm

b. bitumen-bedded tiles of a non-combustible material

c. sand and cement screed, or

d. macadam

Part iv: Pitched roofs covered with bitumen felt

Number of layers	Type of upper layer	Type of underlayer	Deck of 6mm plywood, 12.5mm wood chipboard, 16mm (finished) T&G or 19mm (finished) plain edged timber boarding	Deck of compressed straw slab	Deck or screeded woodwool slab	Profiled fibre reinforced cement or steel deck (single or double skin) with or without fibre insulating board overlay	Profiled aluminium deck (single or double skin) with or without fibre insulating board overlay	Concrete or clay pot slab (insitu or pre-cast)
	Type 1E	Type 1B minimum mass 13kg/10m^2	CC	AC	AC	AC	AC	AB
2 or 3 layers built up in accordance with CP 144: Part 3 1970	Type 2E	Type 1B minimum mass 13kg/10m^2	BB	AB	AB	AB	AB	AB
	Type 2E	Type 2B	AB	AB	AB	AB	AB	AB
	Type 3E	Type 3B or 3G	BC	AC	AB	AB	AB	AB

Note
Any reference in this table to bitumen felt of a specified type is a reference to bitumen felt as so designated in BS 747: 1977.

Part v: Pitched or flat roofs covered with fully supported material

Covering material	Supporting structure	Designation
1. Aluminium sheet 2. Copper sheet 3. Zinc sheet 4. Lead sheet 5. Mastic asphalt 6. Vitreous enamelled steel 7. Lead/tin alloy coated steel sheet 8. Zinc/aluminium alloy coated steel sheet 9. Pre-painted (coil coated) steel sheet including liquid-applied pvc coatings	1. Timber joists and: tongued and grooved boarding, or plain edged boarding	AA*
	2. Steel or timber joists with deck of: woodwool slabs, compressed straw slab, wool chipboard, fibre insulating board, or 9.5mm plywood	AA
	3. Concrete or clay pot slab (insitu or pre-cast) or non-combustible deck of steel, aluminium, or fibre cement (with or without insulation)	AA

Note
* Lead sheet supported by timber joists and plain edged boarding may give a BA designation.

Table A6 **Use of non-combustible materials**

Use	Non-combustible materials
1. ladders referred to in the guidance to BI, paragraph 5.22.	a. Any material which when tested to BS 476: Part 11 does not flame nor cause any rise in temperature on either the centre (specimen) or furnace thermocouples.
2. refuse chutes meeting the provisions in the guidance to B3, paragraph 8.28.	
3. suspended ceilings and their supports where there is provision in the guidance to B3, paragraph 9.13, for them to be constructed of non-combustible materials.	b. Totally inorganic materials such as concrete, fired clay, ceramics, metals, plaster and masonry containing not more than 1 per cent by weight or volume of organic material. (Use in buildings of combustible metals such as magnesium/aluminium alloys should be assessed in each individual case).
4. pipes meeting the provisions in the guidance to B3, Table 15.	
5. flue walls meeting the provisions in the guidance to B3, Diagrams 35.	c. Concrete bricks or blocks meeting BS 6073: Part 1: 1981.
6. construction forming car parks referred to in the guidance to B3, paragraph 11.3.	d. Products classified as non-combustible under BS 476: Part 4: 1970.

Table A7 **Use of materials of limited combustibility**

Use	Materials of limited combustibility
1. stairs where there is provision in the guidance to BI for them to be constructed of materials of limited combustibility (see 5.19).	a. Any non-combustible material listed in Table A6.
2. materials above a suspended ceiling meeting the provisions in the guidance to B3, paragraph 9.13.	b. Any material of density 300 kg/m^3 or more, which when tested to BS 476: Part 11, does not flame and the rise in temperature on the furnace thermocouple is not more than 20°C.
3. reinforcement/support for fire-stopping referred to in the guidance to B3, see 10.13.	c. Any material with a non-combustible core at least 8mm thick having combustible facings (on one or both sides) not more than 0.5mm thick. (Where a flame spread rating is specified, these materials must also meet the appropriate test requirements).
4. roof coverings meeting the provisions:	
a. in the guidance to B3, paragraph 9.11, or	
b. in the guidance to B4, Table 17, or	
c. in the guidance to B4, Diagram 42.	
5. roof deck meeting the provisions of the guidance of B3 Diagram 24a.	
6. class 0 materials meeting the provisions Appendix A, paragraph A12(a).	
7. ceiling tiles or panels of any fire protecting suspended ceiling (Type D) in Table A3.	
8. compartment walls and compartment floors in hospitals referred to in paragraph 8.27	
9. insulation material in external wall construction referred to in paragraph 12.7	Any of the materials (a), (b), or (c) above, or:
10. insulation above any fire-protecting suspended ceiling (Type D) in Table A3.	d. Any material of density less than 300 kg/m^3, which when tested to BS 476: Part 11, does not flame for more than 10 seconds and the rise in temperature on the centre (specimen) thermocouple is not more than 35°C and on the furnace thermocouple is not more than 25°C.

Table A8 **Typical performance ratings of some generic materials and products**

Rating	Material or product
Class 0	1. any non-combustible material or material of limited combustibility. (Composite products listed in Table A7 must meet the test requirements given in paragraph A12(b))
	2. brickwork, blockwork, concrete and ceramic tiles
	3. plasterboard (painted or not, or with a PVC facing not more than 0.5mm thick) with or without an air gap or fibrous or cellular insulating material behind
	4. woodwool cement slabs
	5. mineral fibre tiles or sheets with cement or resin binding
Class 3	6. timber or plywood with a density more than 400 kg/m^3, painted or unpainted
	7. wood particle board or hardboard, either treated or painted
	8. standard glass reinforced polyesters

Notes:

1. Materials and products listed under Class 0 also meet Class 1.

2. Timber products listed under Class 3 can be brought up to Class 1 with appropriate proprietary treatments.

3. The following materials and products may achieve the ratings listed below. However, as the properties of different products with the same generic description vary, the ratings of these materials/products should be substantiated by test evidence.

Class 0   aluminium faced fibre insulating board, flame retardant decorative laminates on a calcium silicate board, thick polycarbonate sheet, phenolic sheet and UPVC;

Class 1   phenolic or melamine laminates on a calcium silicate substrate and flame retardant decorative laminates on a combustible substrate.

Appendix B

FIRE DOORS

B1 All fire doors should have the appropriate performance given in Table BI. In the table doors are identified by their performance under test to BS 476: Part 22, in terms of integrity for a period of minutes, eg FD30. A suffix (S) is added for doors where restricted smoke leakage at ambient temperature is needed. The method of test exposure is from each side of the door separately, except in the case of lift doors which are tested from the landing side only.

B2 All fire doors should be fitted with an automatic self-closing device except for fire doors to cupboards and to service ducts which are normally kept locked shut.

B3 Where a self-closing device would be considered a hindrance to the normal approved use of the building, self-closing fire doors may be held open by:

a. fusible link (but not if the door is fitted in an opening provided as a means of escape unless it complies with paragraph B4); or

b. an automatic release mechanism if the door can also be closed manually and it is not to

i. the only escape stair serving a building (or part of a building), or

ii. a firefighting stair, or

iii. an escape stair serving a building in any Residential purpose group; or

c. a door closure delay device.

B4 Two fire doors may be fitted in the same opening so that the total fire resistance is the sum of their individual fire resistances, provided that each door is capable of closing the opening. In such a case , if the opening is provided as a means of escape, both doors should be self-closing, but one of them may be fitted with an automatic self-closing device and be held open by a fusible link if the other door is capable of being easily opened by hand and has at least 30 minutes fire resistance.

B5 Unless shown to be satisfactory when tested as part of a fire door assembly any hinge on which a fire door is hung should be made entirely from materials having a melting point of at least 800°C.

B6 Hardware used on fire doors can significantly affect performance in fire. Guidance is available in a *"Code of practice for hardware essential to the optimum performance of fire resisting timber doorsets"* published by the Association of Builders' Hardware Manufacturers in 1983.

B7 Except for doors identified in B8 below, all fire doors should be marked with the appropriate fire safety sign complying with BS 5499: Part 1 according to whether the door is:

a. to be kept closed when not in use,

b. to be kept locked when not in use, or

c. held open by an automatic release mechanism

Fire doors to cupboards and to service ducts should be marked on the outside; all other fire doors on both sides.

B8 The following fire doors are not required to comply with B7 above:

a. doors within dwellinghouses,

b. doors to and within flats or maisonettes,

c. bedroom doors in 'Other-residential' premises, and

d. lift entrance doors.

B9 Tables AI and A2 set out the minimum periods of fire resistance for the elements of structure to which performance of some doors is linked. Table A4 sets out limitations on the use of uninsulated glazing in fire doors.

Table B1 **Provisions for fire doors**

Position of door	Minimum fire resistance of door in terms of integrity (minutes)[1]
1. In a compartment wall separating buildings	As for the wall in which door is fitted, but a minimum of 60
2. In a compartment wall: a. if it separates a flat or maisonette from a space in common use,	FD 30S
b. enclosing a protected shaft forming a stairway situated wholly or partly above the adjoining ground in a building used for Flats, Other Residential, Assembly & Recreation, or Office purposes,	FD 30S
c. enclosing a protected shaft forming a stairway not described in (b) above,	Half the period of fire resistance of the wall in which it is fitted but 30 minimum and with suffix S
d. not described in (a), (b) or (c) above.	As for the wall it is fitted in, but add S if the door is used for progressive horizontal evacuation under guidance to B1
3. In a compartment floor	As for the floor in which it is fitted
4. Forming part of the enclosures of: a. a protected stairway (except where described in item 9),	FD 30S
b. lift shaft, or	FD 30
c. service shaft, which does not form a protected shaft in 2(c) above	FD 30
5. Forming part of the enclosures of: a. a protected lobby approach (or protected corridor) to a stairway	FD 30S
b. any other protected corridor	FD 20S
6. Affording access to an external escape route	FD 30
7. Sub-dividing: a. corridors connecting alternative exits,	FD 20S
b. dead-end portions of corridors from the remainder of the corridor	FD 20S
8. Any door: a. within a cavity barrier,	FD 30
b. between a dwellinghouse and a garage,	FD 30
c. forming part of the enclosure to a communal area in sheltered housing.	FD 30S
9. Any door: a. forming part of the enclosures to a protected stairway in a single family dwellinghouse,	FD 20
b. forming part of the enclosure to a protected entrance hall or protected landing in a flat or maisonette,	FD 20
c. within any other fire resisting construction in a dwelling not described elsewhere in this table.	FD 20

Notes
1. To BS 476: Part 22 (or BS 476: Part 8 subject to paragraph A5).

S Unless pressurization techniques complying with BS 5588: Part 4 are used, these doors should also have a leakage rate not exceeding 3m^3/m/hour (head and jambs only) when tested at 25 Pa under BS 476: Section 31.1.

Appendix C

METHODS OF MEASUREMENT

C1 Some form of measurement is an integral part of many of the provisions in this document. Diagrams Cl to C5 show how the various forms of measurement should be made.

Note: See Approved Document B1, paragraph 0.37 for methods of measurement of occupant capacity, travel distance and width of doors, escape routes and stairs, which are specific to means of escape in case of fire.

Diagram C1 Cubic capacity

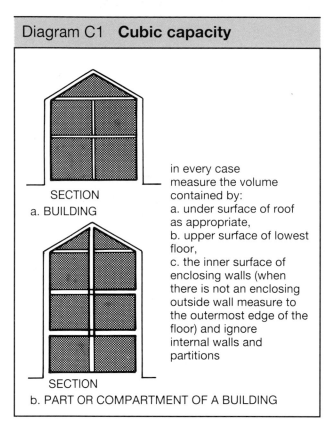

SECTION
a. BUILDING

SECTION
b. PART OR COMPARTMENT OF A BUILDING

in every case measure the volume contained by:
a. under surface of roof as appropriate,
b. upper surface of lowest floor,
c. the inner surface of enclosing walls (when there is not an enclosing outside wall measure to the outermost edge of the floor) and ignore internal walls and partitions

Diagram C2 Area

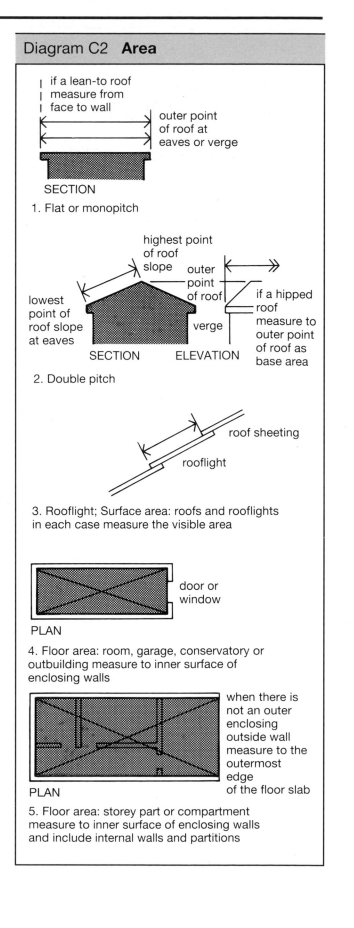

if a lean-to roof measure from face to wall

outer point of roof at eaves or verge

SECTION

1. Flat or monopitch

highest point of roof slope

lowest point of roof slope at eaves

outer point of roof

verge

if a hipped roof measure to outer point of roof as base area

SECTION   ELEVATION

2. Double pitch

roof sheeting

rooflight

3. Rooflight; Surface area: roofs and rooflights in each case measure the visible area

door or window

PLAN

4. Floor area: room, garage, conservatory or outbuilding measure to inner surface of enclosing walls

when there is not an outer enclosing outside wall measure to the outermost edge of the floor slab

PLAN

5. Floor area: storey part or compartment measure to inner surface of enclosing walls and include internal walls and partitions

Diagram C3 **Height**

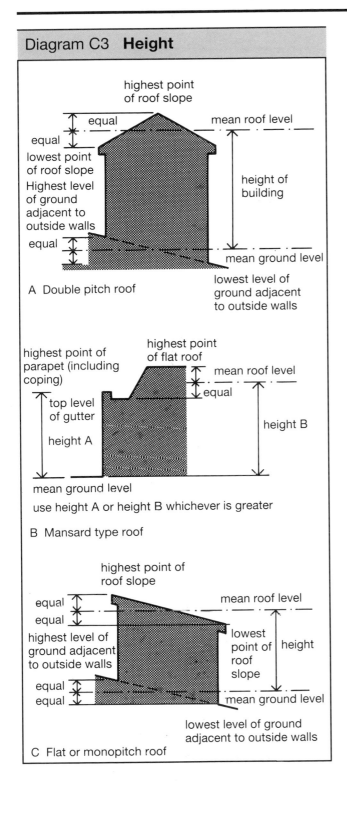

A Double pitch roof

highest point of roof slope

equal / equal

lowest point of roof slope

Highest level of ground adjacent to outside walls

equal

mean roof level

height of building

mean ground level

lowest level of ground adjacent to outside walls

highest point of parapet (including coping)

highest point of flat roof

mean roof level

equal

top level of gutter

height A

height B

mean ground level

use height A or height B whichever is greater

B Mansard type roof

highest point of roof slope

equal / equal

highest level of ground adjacent to outside walls

equal / equal

mean roof level

lowest point of roof slope

height

mean ground level

lowest level of ground adjacent to outside walls

C Flat or monopitch roof

Diagram C4 **Number of storeys**

To count the number of storeys in a building, or in a separated part of a building, count only at the position which gives the greatest number and exclude any basement storeys

building 3 storeys

height of building

2

1

G

basement

mean ground level

1.2m (max)

separated part 3 storeys

separated part 2 storeys

height of part

2

1

G

basement

compart-ment wall

height of part

mean ground level

1.2m (max)

Note

In assembly buildings, a gallery is included as a storey, but not if it is a loading gallery, fly gallery, stage grid, lighting bridge, or any gallery provided for similar purposes, or for maintenance and repair.

In other purpose group buildings, galleries are not counted as a storey.

Diagram C5 **Height of top storey in building**

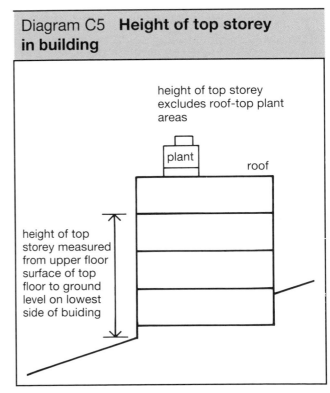

height of top storey excludes roof-top plant areas

plant

roof

height of top storey measured from upper floor surface of top floor to ground level on lowest side of buiding

Appendix D

PURPOSE GROUPS

D1 Many of the provisions in this document are related to the use of the building. The use classifications are termed purpose groups. They can apply to a whole building, or (where a building is compartmented) to a compartment in the building, and the relevant purpose group should be taken from the main use of the building or compartment.

D2 Table D1 sets out the purpose group classification.

Ancillary and main uses

D3 In some situations there may be more than one use involved in a building or compartment, and in certain circumstances it is appropriate to treat the different use as belonging to a purpose group in its own right. These situations are:

a.   where the ancillary use is a flat or maisonette; or

b.   where the ancillary use is of an area that is more than a fifth of the total floor area of the building or compartment; or

c.   storage in a building or compartment of purpose group 4 (shop or commercial) where the storage amounts to more than 1/3rd of the total floor area of the building or compartment.

D4 Some buildings may have two or more main uses that are not ancillary to one another. For example offices over shops from which they are independent. In such cases, each of the uses should be considered as belonging to a purpose group in its own right.

D5 In other cases, and particularly in some large buildings, there may be a complex mix of uses. In such cases it is necessary to consider the possible risk that one part of a complex may have on another and special measures to reduce the risk may be necessary.

Table D1 **Classification of purpose groups**

Title	Group	Purpose for which the building or compartment of a building is intended to be used.
Residential* (dwellings)	1(a)	Flat or maisonette.
	1(b)	Dwellinghouse which contains a habitable storey with a floor level which is more than 4.5m above ground level.
	1(c)	Dwellinghouse which does not contain a habitable storey with a floor level which is more than 4.5m above ground level
Residential (Institutional)	2(a)	Hospital, nursing home, home for old people or for children, school or other similar establishment used as living accommodation or for the treatment, care or maintenance of people suffering from illness or mental or physical disability or handicap, place of detention, where such people sleep on the premises.
(Other)	2(b)	Hotel, boarding house, residential college, hall of residence, hostel, and any other residential purpose not described above.
Office	3	Offices or premises used for the purpose of administration, clerical work (including writing, book keeping, sorting papers, filing, typing, duplicating, machine calculating, drawing and the editorial preparation of matter for publication, police and fire service work), handling money (including banking and building society work), and communications (including postal, telegraph and radio communications) or radio, television, film, audio or video recording, or performance [not open to the public] and their control.
Shop and Commercial	4	Shops or premises used for a retail trade or business (including the sale to members of the public of food or drink for immediate consumption and retail by auction, self-selection and over-the-counter wholesale trading, the business of lending books or periodicals for gain and the business of a barber or hairdresser) and premises to which the public is invited to deliver or collect goods in connection with their hire repair or other treatment, or (except in the case of repair of motor vehicles) where they themselves may carry out such repairs or other treatments.
Assembly and Recreation	5	Place of assembly, entertainment or recreation; including bingo halls, broadcasting, recording and film studios open to the public, casinos, dance halls; entertainment, conference, exhibition and leisure centres; funfairs and amusement arcades; museums and art galleries; non residential clubs, theatres, cinemas and concert halls; educational establishments, dancing schools, gymnasia, swimming pool buildings, riding schools, skating rinks, sports pavilions, sports stadia; law courts; churches and other buildings of worship, crematoria; libraries open to the public, non-residential day centres, clinics, health centres and surgeries; passenger stations and termini for air, rail, road or sea travel; public toilets; zoos and menageries.
Industrial	6	Factories and other premises used for manufacturing, altering, repairing, cleaning, washing, breaking-up, adapting or processing any article; generating power or slaughtering livestock
Storage and other non-residential+	7(a)	Place for the storage or deposit of goods or materials [other than described under 7(b)] and any building not within any of the purpose groups 1 to 6.
	7(b)	Car parks designed to admit and accommodate only cars, motorcycles and passenger or light goods vehicles weighing no more than 2500kg gross.

Notes

*   Includes any surgeries, consulting rooms, offices or other accommodation, not exceeding 50m² in total, forming part of a dwelling and used by an occupant of the dwelling in a professional or business capacity.

+   A detached garage not more than 40m² in area is included in purpose group 1(c); as is a detached open carport of not more than 40m², or a detached building which consists of a garage and open carport where neither the garage nor open carport exceeds 40m² in area.

Appendix E

DEFINITIONS

Access room A room through which passes the only escape route from an inner room.

Accommodation stair A stair, additional to that or those required for escape purposes, provided for the convenience of occupants.

Alternative escape routes Escape routes sufficiently separated by either direction and space, or by fire-resisting construction, to ensure that one is still available should the other be affected by fire. (N.B. A second stair, balcony or flat roof which enables a person to reach a place free from danger from fire, is considered an alternative escape route for the purposes of a dwellinghouse).

Alternative exit One of two or more exits, each of which is separate from the other.

Appliance ventilation duct A duct provided to convey combustion air to a gas appliance.

Atrium (plural atria) A vertical space within a building, (other than a shaft used solely for stairs, escalators, lifts or services), openly connecting three or more storeys and enclosed at the top by a floor or roof.

Automatic release mechanism A device which will allow a door held open by it to close automatically in the event of each or any one of the following:

a. detection of smoke by automatic apparatus suitable in nature, quality and location;

b. operation of a hand operated switch fitted in a suitable position;

c. failure of electricity supply to the device, apparatus or switch;

d. operation of the fire alarm system if any.

Automatic self-closing device Does not include rising butt hinges unless the door is:

a. to (or within) a dwelling;

b. between a dwellinghouse and its garage; or

c. in a cavity barrier.

Basement storey A storey with a floor which at some point is more than 1.2m below the highest level of ground adjacent to the outside walls. (However, see Appendix A, Table A2, for situations where the storey is considered to be a basement only because of a sloping site).

Boundary The boundary of the land belonging to the building, or where the land abuts a road, railway, canal or river, the centreline of that road, railway, canal or river. (See Diagram 37).

Cavity barrier A construction provided to close a concealed space against penetration of smoke or flame, or provided to restrict the movement of smoke or flame within such a space.

Ceiling A part of a building which encloses and is exposed overhead in a room, protected shaft or circulation space. (The soffit of a rooflight is included as part of the surface of the ceiling, but not the frame. An upstand below a rooflight would be considered as wall).

Circulation space A space (including a protected stairway) mainly used as a means of access between a room and an exit from the building or compartment.

Class 0 A product performance classification for wall and ceiling linings. The relevant test criteria are set out in Appendix A, paragraph A12.

Common balcony A walkway, open to the air on one or more sides, forming part of the escape route from more than one flat or maisonette.

Common stair An escape stair serving more than one flat or maisonette.

Compartment (fire) A building or part of a building, comprising one or more rooms, spaces or storeys, constructed to prevent the spread of fire to or from another part of the same building, or an adjoining building. (A roof space above the top storey of a compartment is included in that compartment). (See also Separated part).

Compartment wall or floor A fire-resisting wall/floor used in the separation of one fire compartment from another. (Constructional provisions are given in Section 8)

Concealed space or cavity A space enclosed by elements of a building (including a suspended ceiling) or contained within an element, but not a room, cupboard, circulation space, protected shaft or space within a flue, chute, duct, pipe or conduit.

Conservatory A single storey part of a building where the roof and walls are substantially glazed with a transparent or translucent material.

Corridor access A design of a building containing flats in which each dwelling is approached via a common horizontal internal access or circulation space which may include a common entrance hall.

Dead-end Area from which escape is possible in one direction only.

Direct distance The shortest distance from any point within the floor area, measured within the external enclosures of the building, to the nearest storey exit ignoring walls, partitions and fittings, other than the enclosing walls/partitions to protected stairways.

Dwelling a unit of residential accommodation occupied (whether or not as a sole or main residence):

a.   by a single person or by people living together as a family; or

b.   by not more than 6 residents living together as a single household, including a household where care is provided for residents.

Element of structure -

a.   a member forming part of the structural frame of a building or any other beam or column;

b.   a loadbearing wall or loadbearing part of a wall;

c.   a floor;

d.   a gallery;

e.   an external wall, and

f.   a compartment wall (including a wall common to two or more buildings). (However, see the guidance to B3, paragraph 7.4, for exclusions from the provisions for elements of structure).

Emergency lighting Lighting provided for use when the supply to the normal lighting fails.

Escape lighting That part of the emergency lighting which is provided to ensure that the escape route is illuminated at all material times.

Escape route Route forming that part of the means of escape from any point in a building to a final exit.

Evacuation lift A lift that may be used for the evacuation of disabled people in a fire.

External wall (or side of a building) includes a part of a roof pitched at an angle of more than 70° to the horizontal, if that part of the roof adjoins a space within the building to which persons have access (but not access only for repair or maintenance).

Final exit The termination of an escape route from a building giving direct access to a street, passageway, walkway or open space, and sited to ensure the rapid dispersal of persons from the vicinity of a building so that they are no longer in danger from fire and/or smoke.

Fire door A door or shutter, provided for the passage of persons, air or objects, which together with its frame and furniture as installed in a building, is intended (when closed) to resist the passage of fire and/or gaseous products of combustion, and is capable of meeting specified performance criteria to those ends. (It may have one or more leaves, and the term includes a cover or other form of protection to an opening in a fire-resisting wall or floor, or in a structure surrounding a protected shaft).

Fire-resisting (fire resistance) the ability of a component or construction of a building to satisfy for a stated period of time, some or all of the appropriate criteria specified in the relevant Part of BS 476.

Fire stop A seal provided to close an imperfection of fit or design tolerance between elements or components, to restrict the passage of fire and smoke.

Firefighting lift A lift designed to have additional protection, with controls that enable it to be used under the direct control of the fire service in fighting a fire. (See Sections 15-18)..

Firefighting lobby A protected lobby providing access from a firefighting stair to the accommodation area and to any associated firefighting lift.

Firefighting shaft A protected enclosure containing a firefighting stair, firefighting lobbies and, if provided, a firefighting lift, together with its machine room.

Firefighting stair A protected stair communicating with the accommodation area only through a firefighting lobby.

Gallery A floor, including a raised storage area, which is less than one-half of the area of the space into which it projects.

Habitable room A room used, or intended to be used, for dwelling purposes (including for the purposes of Part B, a kitchen, but not a bathroom).

Height (of a building or storey for the purposes of Part B) Height of a building is measured as shown in Appendix C, Diagram C3, and height of the floor of the a top storey above ground is measured as shown in Appendix C, Diagram C5.

Inner room Room from which escape is possible only by passing through another room (the access room).

Material of limited combustibility A material performance specification that includes noncombustible materials, and for which the relevant test criteria are set out in Appendix A, paragraph A8.

Means of escape Structural means whereby [in the event of fire] a safe route or routes is or are provided for persons to travel from any point in a building to a place of safety.

Measurement area, cubic capacity, height of a building and number of storeys, see Appendix C, Diagrams Cl to C5; occupant capacity, travel distance, and width of a doorway, escape route and a stair, see paragraph 0.37.

Non-combustible material The highest level of reaction to fire performance. The relevant test criteria are set out in Appendix A, paragraph A7.

Notional boundary A boundary presumed to exist between buildings on the same site (see Section 13, Diagram 38). The concept is applied only to buildings in the residential and the assembly and recreation purpose groups.

Open spatial planning The internal arrangement of a building in which more than one storey or level is contained in one undivided volume, eg split-level floors. For the purposes of this document there is a distinction between open spatial planning and an atrium space.

Perimeter (of building) The maximum aggregate plan perimeter, found by vertical projection onto a horizontal plane (see Section 16, Diagram 43).

Pipe (for the purposes of Section 10) - includes pipe fittings and accessories; and excludes a flue pipe and a pipe used for ventilating purposes (other than a ventilating pipe for an above ground drainage-system).

Places of special fire risk Oil-filled transformer and switchgear rooms, boiler rooms, storage space for fuel or other highly flammable substances, and rooms housing a fixed internal combustion engine.

Platform floor (access or raised floor) A floor supported by a structural floor, but with an intervening concealed space which is intended to house services.

Pressurization A method of protecting escape routes against the ingress of smoke by maintaining an air pressure difference between the protected area and adjoining accommodation.

Protected circuit An electrical circuit protected against fire

Protected corridor/lobby A corridor or lobby which is adequately protected from fire in adjoining accommodation by fire-resisting construction.

Protected entrance hall/landing A circulation area consisting of a hall or space in a dwelling, enclosed with fire-resisting construction (other than any part which is an external wall of a building) .

Protected shaft A shaft which enables persons, air or objects to pass from one compartment to another, and which is enclosed with fire-resisting construction.

Protected stairway A stair discharging through a final exit to a place of safety (including any exit passageway between the foot of the stair and the final exit) that is adequately enclosed with fire-resisting construction.

Purpose group A classification of a building according to the purpose to which it is intended to be put. See Appendix D, Table Dl.

Relevant boundary The boundary which the side of the building faces, (and/or coincides with) and which is parallel, or at an angle of not more than 80°, to the side of the building (see Section 13 Diagram 37). A notional boundary can be a relevant boundary.

Rooflight A domelight, lantern light, skylight, ridge light, glazed barrel vault or other element intended to admit daylight through a roof.

Room (for the purposes of B2) An enclosed space within a building that is not used solely as a circulation space. (The term includes not only conventional rooms, but also cupboards that are not fittings, and large spaces such as warehouses, and auditoria. The term does not include voids such as ducts, ceiling voids and roof spaces).

Separated part (of a building) A form of compartmentation in which a part of a building is separated from another part of the same building by a compartment wall. The wall runs the full height of the part, and is in one vertical plane. (See paras 8.4 and 8.21, and Appendix C, Diagram C4.)

Single storey building A building consisting of a ground storey only. (A separated part which consists of a ground storey only, with a roof to which access is only provided for repair or maintenance, may be treated as a single storey building). Basements are not included in counting the number of storeys in a building (see Appendix C)

Storey includes:

a. any gallery in an assembly building (purpose group 5); and

b. any gallery in any other type of building if its area is more than half that of the space into which it projects; and

c. a roof, unless it is accessible only for maintenance and repair.

Storey exit A final exit, or a doorway giving direct access into a protected stairway, firefighting lobby, or external escape route. (N.B. A door in a compartment wall in a hospital is considered as a storey exit for the purposes of B1, see paragraph 3.28).

Suspended ceiling (fire-protecting) A ceiling suspended below a floor, which contributes to the fire resistance of the floor. Appendix A, Table A3, classifies different types of suspended ceiling.

Thermoplastic material See Appendix A, paragraph A16.

Travel distance (unless otherwise specified, eg. as in the case of flats) The actual distance to be travelled by a person from any point within the floor area to the nearest storey exit, having regard to the layout of walls, partitions and fittings.

Unprotected area In relation to a side or external wall of a building means:

a. window, door or other opening; and

b. any part of the external wall which has less than the relevant fire resistance set out in Section 12; and

c. any part of the external wall which has combustible material more than 1mm thick attached or applied to its external face, whether for cladding or any other purpose. (Combustible material in this context is any material that is not included in Tables A6 or A7 in Appendix A).

Standards referred to

Introduction
BS 5588: *Fire precautions in the design , construction and use of buildings:*
Part 10: 1991 *Code of practice for enclosed shopping complexes*

B1 Sections 1-5
BS 5266: *Emergency lighting:*
Part 1: 1988 *Code of practice for the emergency lighting of premises other than cinemas and certain other specified premises used for entertainment.*

BS 5306: *Fire extinguishing installations and equipment on premises:*
Part 2: 1990 *Specification for sprinkler systems.*

BS 5395: *Stairs, ladders and walkways:*
Part 2: 1984 *Code of practice for the design of helical and spiral stairs*
Amendment slip
1: AMD 6076.

BS 5446: *Specification for components of automatic fire alarm systems for residential purposes:*
Part 1: 1990 *Point-type smoke detectors.*

BS 5499: *Fire safety signs, notices and graphic symbols:*
Part 1: 1990 *Specification for fire safety signs.*

BS 5588: *Fire precautions in the design, construction and use of buildings:*
Part 1: 1990 *Code of practice for residential buildings.*
Part 2: 1985 *Code of practice for shops*
Amendment slips
1: AMD 5555,
2: AMD 6239,
3: AMD 6478.
Part 3: 1983 *Code of practice for office buildings*
Amendment slips
1: AMD 5556,
2: AMD 5825,
3: AMD 6160.
Part 4: 1978 *Code of practice for smoke control in protected escape routes using pressurization*
Amendment slip
1: AMD 5377.
Part 5: 1991 *Code of practice for firefighting stairs and lifts.*
Part 6: 1991 *Code of practice for assembly buildings.*
Part 8: 1988 *Code of practice for means of escape for disabled people.*
Part 9: 1989 *Code of practice for ventilation and air conditioning ductwork.*
Part 10: 1991 *Code of practice for enclosed shopping complexes.*

BS 5720: 1979 *Code of practice for mechanical ventilation and air conditioning in buildings.*

BS 5839: *Fire detection and alarm systems for buildings:*

Part 1: 1988 *Code of practice for system design, installation and servicing.*

BS 5906: 1980 *Code of practice for storage and onsite treatment of solid waste from buildings.*

BS 6387: 1983 *Specification for performance requirements for cables required to maintain circuit integrity under fire conditions*
Amendment slips
1: AMD 4989,
2: AMD 5615.

CP 1007: 1955 *Maintained lighting for cinemas.*

B2. Section 6
BS 476: *Fire tests on building materials and structures:*
Part 6: 1981 *Method of test for fire propagation for products.*
Part 6: 1989 *Method of test for fire propagation for products.*
Part 7: 1971 *Surface spread of flame test for materials.*
Part 7: 1987 *Method for classification of the surface spread of flame of products*
Amendment slip
1: AMD 6249.

B3. Sections 7-11
BS 4514: 1983 *Specification for unplasticized PVC soil and ventilating pipes, fittings and accessories*
Amendment slips
1: AMD 4517,
2: AMD 5584.

BS 5255: 1989 *Specification for thermoplastics waste pipe and fittings.*

BS 5306: *Fire extinguishing installations and equipment on premises:*
Part 2: 1990 *Specification for sprinkler systems*

BS 5588: *Fire precautions in the design, construction and use of buildings:*
Part 5: 1991 *Code of practice for firefighting stairs and lifts.*
Part 9: 1989 *Code of practice for ventilation and air conditioning ductwork.*
Part 10: 1991 *Code of practice for enclosed shopping complexes.*

B4. Sections 12-14
BS 476: *Fire tests on building materials and structures:*
Part 3: 1958 *External fire exposure roof tests.*
Part 6: 1981 *Method of test for fire propagation for products.*
Part 6: 1989 *Method of test for fire propagation for products.*

BS 5306: *Fire extinguishing installations and equipment on premises:*
Part 2: 1990 *Sprinkler systems.*

B5. Sections 15-18

BS 5306: *Fire extinguishing installations and equipment on premises:*

Part 1: 1976 (1988) *Hydrant systems, hose reels and foam inlets*
Amendment slips
1: AMD 4649,
2: AMD 5756.
Part 2: 1990 *Specification for sprinkler systems.*

BS 5588: *Fire precautions in the design, construction and use of buildings:*
Part 5: 1991 *Code of practice for firefighting stairs and lifts.*
Part 10: 1991 *Code of practice for enclosed shopping complexes.*

Appendix A

BS 476: *Fire tests on building materials and structures:*
Part 3 : 1958 *External fire exposure roof tests.*
Part 4 : 1970 (1984) *Non-combustibility test for materials*
Amendment slips
1: AMD 2483,
2: AMD 4390.
Part 6: 1981 *Method of test for fire propagation for products.*
Part 6: 1989 *Method of test for fire propagation for products.*
Part 7: 1971 *Surface spread of flame tests for materials.*
Part 7: 1987 *Method for classification of the surface spread of flame of products*
Amendment slip
1: AMD 6249.
Part 8: 1972 *Test methods and criteria for the fire resistance of elements of building construction*
Amendment slips
1: AMD 1873,
2: AMD 3816,
3: AMD 4822.
Part 11: 1982 *Method for assessing the heat emission from building products.*
Part 20: 1987 *Method for determination of the fire resistance of elements of construction (general principles)*
Amendment slip
1: AMD 6487.
Part 21: 1987 *Methods for determination of the fire resistance of loadbearing elements of construction.*
Part 22: 1987 *Methods for determination of the fire resistance of non-loadbearing elements of construction.*
Part 23: 1987 *Methods for determination of the contribution of components to the fire resistance of a structure.*
Part 24: 1987 *Method for determination of the fire resistance of ventilation ducts.*

BS 747: 1977: *Specification for roofing felts*
Amendment slips
1: AMD 3775,
2: AMD 4609,
3: AMD 5101.

BS 2782: 1970 *Methods of testing plastics:* Part 1: *Thermal properties:*
Method 120A *Determination of the Vicat softening temperature for thermoplastics*
Part 5: *Miscellaneous methods:*
Method 508A

BS 5306: *Fire extinguishing installations and equipment on premises:*
Part 2: 1990 *Specification for sprinkler systems*

BS 5438: 1976 *Methods of test for flammability of vertically oriented textile fabrics and fabric assemblies subjected to a small igniting flame:*
Test 2: 1989

BS 5867 *Specification for fabrics for curtains and drapes:*

Part 2: 1980 *Flammability requirements*
Amendment slip
1: AMD 4319.

BS 6073 *Precast concrete masonry units*
Part 1: 1981 *Specification for precast concrete masonry units*
Amendment slips
1: AMD 3944,
2: AMD 4462.

BS 6336: 1982 *Guide to development and presentation of fire tests and their use in hazard assessment.*

CP 144: *Roof coverings:*
Part 3: 1970. *Built-up bitumen felt*
Amendment slips
1: AMD 2527,
2: AMD 5229.

PD 6520: 1988 *Guide to fire test methods for building materials and elements of construction*

Appendix B

BS 476: *Fire tests on building materials and structures:*

Part 8: 1972 *Test methods and criteria for the fire resistance of elements of building construction*
Amendment slips
1: AMD 1873,
2: AMD 3816,
3: AMD 4822.
Part 22: 1987 *Methods for determination of the fire resistance of non-loadbearing elements of construction.*

Part 31: *Methods for measuring smoke penetration through doorsets and shutter assemblies:*
Section 31.1: 1983 *Measurement under ambient temperature conditions.*

BS 5499: *Fire safety signs, notices and graphic symbols:*
Part 1: 1990 *Specification for fire safety signs.*

BS 5588 *Fire precautions in the design, construction and use of buildings*
Part 4: 1978. *Code of practice for smoke control in protected escape routes using pressurization*
Amendment slip
1: AMD 5377.

Other publications referred to

Approved Document B1

The Building Regulations 1991. Approved Document K. Stairs, ramps and guards. (DOE/Welsh Office) HMSO, Approved Document M Access and facilities for disabled people, Approved Document N Glazing - materials and protection.

"Wake up! Get a smoke alarm" Home Office booklet FB2, HMSO 1990.

Design principles for smoke ventilation in enclosed shopping centres. BR 186/1990 (Revision of Smoke control methods in enclosed shopping complexes of one or more storeys. A design summary. (BRE) HMSO, 1979)

Draft guide to fire precautions in existing hospitals. Home Office 1982

Draft guide to fire precautions in existing residential care premises Home Office/Scottish Home and Health Dept. 1983

Firecode. HTM 81. Fire precautions in new hospitals. (DHSS) HMSO, 1987.

Firecode. HTM 88. Guide to Fire Precautions in NHS housing in the Community for mentally handicapped (or mentally ill) people.

Firecode. Nucleus fire precautions recommendations (D or H) HMSO, 1989.

Building Bulletin 7. Fire and the design of educational buildings. (DES) HMSO, 1988.

Joint circular DOE, Home Office and Welsh Office. Memorandum on overcrowding and houses in multiple occupation. Circular 12/86 (DOE), 39/86 (Home Office), 23/86 (Welsh Office) HMSO 1986.

Gas Safety Regulations 1972 (SI 1972 No. 1178)

Gas Safety (Installation & Use) Regulations 1984, as amended 1990 (SI. 1984 No. 1358)

Fire Precautions Act 1971. Guide to fire precautions in existing places of work that require a fire certificate: Factories, offices, shops and railway premises. HMSO 1989

Guide to Safety at Sports Grounds. Home Office/Scottish Office HMSO 1990

Approved Document B3

Design principles for smoke ventilation in enclosed shopping centres. BR 186/1990.

(Revision of Smoke control methods in enclosed shopping complexes of one or more storeys. A design summary. (BRE) HMSO, 1979)-

Gas Safety Regulations 1972 (SI 1972 No. 1178)

Gas Safety (Installation and Use) Regulations 1984, as amended 1990 (SI. 1984 No. 1358 and SI. 1990 No. 824)

Approved Document B4

External fire spread: Building separation and boundary distances, BRE 187, 1991.

The Building Regulations 1985 Approved Document B2/3/4 (DOE/Welsh Office) 1985 edition

Fire and steel construction: The behaviour of steel portal frames in boundary conditions, 1990 2nd edition (available from the Steel Construction Institute, Silwood Park, Ascot, Berks, SL5 7QN).

Appendix A

Guidelines for the construction of structural elements. BR 128 BRE, 1988.

Increasing the fire resistance of existing timber floors. BRE Digest 208, 1988.

Fire test results on building products: fire resistance. FPA, 1983.

Rules for the construction and installation of firebreak doors and shutters. LPC, 1988.

Fire protection for structural steel in buildings. (Second edition) ASFPCM, 1988.

Appendix B

Code of practice for hardware essential to the optimum performance of timber doorsets ABHM 1983.

Index

Printed in the United Kingdom for The Stationery Office
J32633 C30 12/97 009091

HAVERING COLLEGE OF F & H E

159654

7 DAY BOOK

WITHDRAWN 14-2-22